Love Potions for Healthy
Relationships
A Series

Pungent Boundaries

Nancy Landrum, M.A.

authorHOUSE®

AuthorHouse™
1663 Liberty Drive
Bloomington, IN 47403
www.authorhouse.com
Phone: 1-800-839-8640

Illustrations by Nancy Landrum
Cover Design by Michelle Owens of Stratatomic

Published by AuthorHouse 03/12/2015

ISBN: 978-1-4969-4433-7 (sc)
ISBN: 978-1-4969-4434-4 (e)

Print information available on the last page.

This book is printed on acid-free paper.

DESCRIPTION of the Series: *Love Potions for Healthy Relationships*
Nancy Landrum has written a series of transformational books that deliver lightning bolts of insight! Each volume in the series covers a particular ingredient present in a healthy relationship. These powerful truths will demystify how healthy relationships work. Her wisdom is harvested from a passionate, lifetime quest for the secret to loving and being loved. The examples from her years of relationship coaching make reading these volumes engaging as well as inspiring. Each chapter ends with perceptive recipes to help the reader add that particular ingredient to his or her love potion.

In ***Pungent Boundaries***, the fourth volume of her ***Love Potions for Healthy Relationships*** series, Nancy Landrum uses many descriptions and examples to clarify the sometimes confusing topic of codependency and boundary setting. Nancy's life experience uniquely qualifies her to educate others about the concepts and pitfalls of setting healthy boundaries. If you're tired of feeling resentful, exhausted from trying to figure out what is wrong, struggling to understand the difference between loving support and unhealthy codependency, this simply written handbook is for you. By learning to establish, and maintain, healthy boundaries, your life will be liberated from resentment that poisons your relationships and prevents you from taking good care of *yourself.*

Other *Love Potions for Healthy Relationships* Volumes:

Season the Pot: Uncovers the powerful role of unconscious beliefs in determining the quality of our relationships. Copyright 2013

Communication Elixirs: Defines common communication methods that always damage a relationship and teaches simple communication skills that enable each person to be heard and understood. Copyright 2013

Savory Safeguards: Teaches practical strategies for managing strong emotions as well as a creative, powerful problem solving process. Copyright 2014.

Pungent Boundaries: Reveals how to establish, and maintain, healthy boundaries to liberate one's relationships from resentments. Copyright 2014.

Winning Strategies for Stepfamilies: Maps out research based strategies with real-life examples that are needed to navigate the unique dynamics of step-families.

Sweeten the Potion: Illumines the transformative power of adding thoughtfulness, appreciation, love languages and romance (when appropriate) to your relationships.

Elegantly Bottle Your Potion: A view from the top; what grand purposes relationships serve in our growth as human beings.

DEDICATION

For Steven
You gave me thousands of delightful memories and
Taught me more about Codependency and Boundaries
than I thought I needed to know.
I look forward to my next big hug from you!

I am grateful beyond words to:

My Clients
I am continually awed by the trust you place in me.
Every step forward in your relationships gives
me energy to continue this work.

To Paul, Kristi, and Traci
Your careful reading, suggestions and edits to this series
have made the final product so much better!

TABLE OF CONTENTS

LOVE POTIONS SERIES INTRODUCTION

The definition of a potion is: a drink or draft reputed to have medicinal, poisonous or magical powers. In this series, "potion" refers to any ingredient that influences the quality of a relationship. Many of us, without intending to, have contributed potions to our relationships that cause those relationships to be somewhat distasteful, unsatisfying, bitter, or even dangerous.

Being in a healthy relationship is somewhat like savoring a warm, flavorful concoction when coming in from the cold. Each ingredient or spice alone may taste flat, or even bitter, but the combination of ingredients makes a tasty, healing, and satisfying potion. I believe it's a universal desire to enjoy healthy relationship potions that fulfill our longing for loving and being loved.

Research has provided ample supporting evidence that satisfying relationships are medicinal by contributing to health in many areas of life. Just a few of the areas include physical and mental health, longevity, educational and financial levels achieved, job productivity and stability, and general life-satisfaction. In addition, a stable, loving relationship between a child's parents has been shown to contribute positively to physical and emotional health, school performance, educational level reached, and the success of a child's relationships in adulthood.

The *Love Potions for Healthy Relationships* series is based on the potent ingredients found by my late husband Jim and me when we were searching for help for our failing marriage. In addition, I found these ingredients to be essential in relationship with my children and with every other significant relationship I enjoy. Other ingredients were incorporated as I navigated a painful, but ultimately rich journey with a drug-addicted son.

You can focus on one ingredient at a time, and while you learn about it, think about what flavor it may add to your relationship. Then, if you choose, add it to your own *Love Potion* and move on to another ingredient. The books do not need to be read in their original order. Pick up the one that sparks your interest and dive in.

From both my personal and professional coaching experience, I know that each ingredient can be integrated into the most disturbed relationships with amazingly positive results. Some of the ingredients you may find easy to add. Other ingredients may require far more effort and persistence, stretching you to your limit. But by adding each of these ingredients into your relationships, my hope is that you, like me, will strengthen loving connections and build the healthy relationships for which we all long.

Caution: Not all relationships can be made healthy. We ultimately have control over making only our half of a relationship as healthy as possible. In some cases, you may continue to love someone, but must eliminate or limit your contact with that person. A potion for these strategies is covered in *Pungent Boundaries.*

There is, however, a mysterious dynamic that is often the result when one person is willing to introduce healthier ingredients into a relationship. The other person frequently responds positively. Just as anger usually begets anger, healthier loving is often reciprocated in kind.

Healing is every bit as powerful and transforming, as well, when it only happens within yourself. The potions in this series will help *you* experience the rewards of healthier relationships. And the healthier *you* are, the more apt you are to attract healthier persons into your life and be sensitized to recognize persons who are less prepared for a healthy relationship.

Each volume includes examples from my personal experiences, as well as stories of others whom I've coached or taught. Pertinent quotes and concepts are added from gifted thinkers whom I respect.

Every chapter ends with questions to stimulate your thinking or exercises to help you incorporate what each section teaches about relationships. The exercises are referred to as "Stir the Pot." These chapter-ending suggestions can be applied several ways. One is to do the exercises privately, perhaps in a journal. Second, you may share these ideas with a reading group or with trusted friends. This option will likely increase your ability to successfully create **Love Potions for Healthy Relationships**! Finally, if you want to take the learning even further, either personally or in a group, you are invited to go to my web site to download the work pages recommended in this, and other **Love Potions** volumes. (See section titled *YOU ARE INVITED...*)

Note: My story with Jim, and the lessons we learned in the recovery of our marriage, are described in my first two books that were written with him prior to this current series. (See *ABOUT NANCY'S WORK*.) Several examples in the **Love Potions** books feature our experiences as well. For many years we taught a class together where we were quite vulnerable in sharing examples from our relationship, both failures and successes. In this, and other writings, I only use examples for which I have Jim's prior permission and illustrations we agreed to make public.

You have my admiration and support as you choose ingredients to create your own fragrant and powerful **Love Potion!**

Nancy Landrum

Preview: PUNGENT BOUNDARIES

The whole confusing topic of boundaries begins with our understanding of love and responsibility. What does it really mean to love someone? To act in loving ways? What is my responsibility in this situation or with this person? And what is the other person's responsibility? Although boundary issues have been around since the beginning of relationships, the past several decades have accelerated our understanding with the growing knowledge about the role of codependency in addictive behaviors. The best definition of codependency I've ever heard is "an imbalance of responsibility." (From the course, *The Third Option*, a support program for couples in crisis created by Patricia Crane Ennis, M.S.W.)

An imbalance of responsibility means that one person assumes too much responsibility while another (with whom he/she is in relationship) assumes too little. The need for a boundary is borne out of the frustration generated by this imbalance. Usually the one who has been carrying too much responsibility is the one who is first aware of the need for a boundary that corrects the balance. (Although, I've had a few clients who were relieved to set boundaries for an interfering or disrespectful parent, sibling or friend who wanted too much inappropriate control!)

Learning about boundaries—when to set them and how to enforce them—has been a life-long curriculum for me. The learning began in my late-twenties when I hired a carpenter to build some cabinets in my sewing room. The first few days he was diligent and made quick headway. Then several days went by when I didn't hear from him. I called. He said he'd gotten another job and would get back to finish mine in a few days. I just said, "O.K."

Each time he said he'd come, I'd stay home all day, waiting. No call. No apology. No explanation. The pattern of his promises and no-shows, and my patient responses, lasted for *nine* long months.

At first, I felt self-righteous because I was being so kind. I thought I was demonstrating loving behavior. But then I began to feel angry! A crisis was brewing between what I saw as my value of being a kind person and my desire to have a finished sewing room!

Eventually, the crisis was resolved when I realized that I was participating in his irresponsible behavior by meekly going along with it. This was *not* a loving or even a kind thing to do. Making it easy for him to be irresponsible was, in fact, very unloving!

After a few days of thinking through this revolutionary new thought, I was ready to call him. I asked, "When is the first possible day you could be finished with my job?" He answered, "Next Wednesday." I replied, "In that case, (see the boundary being set here) for every day after Wednesday that my job is not finished, I will subtract $20 from the balance I owe you."

He was incensed! I was calm, respectful and firm. The cabinets were finished the following Monday! He was surly. I was polite and kind. And I'd learned my first lesson about codependency and gained an expanded understanding of what it means to be loving.

In the sewing room lesson, I had assumed full responsibility for his behavior by neglecting to take full responsibility for my need for a timely, completed job. The consequence to me was resentment, frustration, and months without my cabinets. The consequence to him was nine months of positive reinforcement for his lying and irresponsibility.

I've since learned that many times when I feel resentment, it's because I want a person to be more responsible in his or her behavior toward me. The truth is that often I am unwilling to take full responsibility for myself...my feelings, my needs. I'm virtually saying, "You change! I don't want to." Resentment is a warning flag that says, "It's time to grow. Time to change how you're looking at this or handling this. Time to become more self-responsible."

This is not easy stuff! Sorting out responsibilities, setting limits and enforcing healthy boundaries takes incredible strength! It's graduate level relationship coursework. It doesn't feel warm and fuzzy and loving. Boundary setting is, in fact, rather *pungent* work!

The definitions of pungent are:

1. Sharply affecting the organs of taste or smell, as if by a penetrating power; biting; acrid;
2. Acutely distressing to the feelings or mind; poignant;
3. Caustic, biting, or sharply expressive, such as pungent remarks;
4. Mentally stimulating or appealing, such as pungent wit;
5. In biology, piercing or sharp-pointed.

The resentment, or even rage, that is generated when I am expected to clean up someone else's mess, stinks! When my love for someone is at war with my desire to see him assume appropriate responsibility for himself, I feel acutely distressed. Sometimes my choice to set a healthy boundary results in her accusing me of being hard, caustic, unfair or even unloving. There's no doubt that when a healthy boundary is introduced into what has been a co-dependent relationship, it can feel piercing or sharp-pointed to both parties. But, as definition #4 says, getting clear about my personal responsibility and setting an appropriate, healthy boundary for another's behavior toward me, is definitely mentally stimulating and the result is truly appealing!

Getting clear about which responsibilities are mine and which ones belong to the other person is foundational for healthy self-love and love for another. It is impossible to be genuinely, truly loving to another if I am not taking appropriate care of myself. As with the carpenter illustration above, it is *never* loving to give my active or passive support to the unhealthy or self-destructive behaviors of another. In fact, because healthy relationship laws are so amazingly fair, when I make a decision that is *genuinely* in my best interests, it will automatically be best for the other person, as well, whether or not that choice is welcomed.

If that last statement blows your mind; if you're tired of feeling taken advantage of; tired of living with chronic resentment; tired of carrying the load created by another's behavior; and ready to assume responsibility for healthy change, you've picked up the right book at the right time!

Let the lessons begin!

Chapter 1: A KALEIDOSCOPE

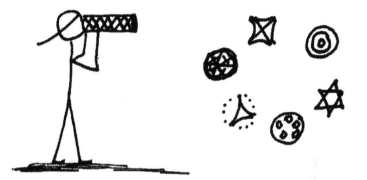

Merriam-Webster online dictionary defines "kaleidoscope" as "a tube that has mirrors and loose pieces of colored glass or plastic inside at one end so that you see many different patterns when you turn the tube while looking in through the other end." The patterns look like multiple variations on a snowflake or the most intricate mandala or mosaic designs. I imagine that most of us have been intrigued by the changing patterns and shapes created in a kaleidoscope.

A book about boundaries cannot be written without including the relationship pattern of codependency. Codependent persons are frequently in relationship with those practicing an addiction, who have a need to control, who tend to be dependent, or demonstrate narcissistic (self-centered) patterns of behavior. The characteristics of a relationship between a person with codependent tendencies and any of the above personalities, often creates great distress. The primary way out of the distress is for the codependent to set, and enforce, effective boundaries.

Even as I write these words I can hear some of you asking, "But what *is* codependency? Am I being codependent? How do I know when a boundary is needed? What does this topic have to do with the conflicts I'm having with _____? How will this volume help me create a healthy love potion?"

And that describes my challenge as an author. Codependency and boundary setting are slippery topics. It's hard to get a grip on them because they are intermixed with words such as control, lack of control, choices, consequences, approval, helping, caring, expectations, resentment, love, pity, shame, responsibility, irresponsibility, drama, addictions, judgments, rejection, training, life lessons, beliefs, behaviors, fear, denial, and more. Right now it's as though the pieces of this topic are scattered all over the table rather than creating the orderly, symmetrical patterns in a kaleidoscope.

I've designed this book so that each chapter will give you a different view of codependency and boundary setting. It's as though after reading Chapter 1, you turn the kaleidoscope slightly and a different pattern is seen even though it's created by the same pieces of glass or plastic. Then, after reading Chapter 2, you turn the kaleidoscope again, and see the same pieces making a different pattern. All the chapters are using the same pieces but each chapter presents them in a different configuration.

My goal is to describe and illustrate codependency and boundary setting in so many ways that you, the reader, will relate to a story, a description, a feeling, or a pattern of behavior in one or more of these chapters or examples. As a result, you'll have more clarity about what codependence is and how codependency may be creating unnecessary stress in your life. You will also be more confident in the setting of appropriate boundaries. As I write each chapter I imagine hearing your "ah-hahs" or seeing light bulbs illuminating your mind!

HISTORY
Codependency as a behavioral pattern was first identified in the alcohol addiction recovery movement more than fifty years ago. In the beginning it was called co-alcoholism because it was first identified as a common behavior pattern of persons in relationship with an alcoholic. The co-part of the word indicates that it takes two to create this condition. You'll be reading about the role of each person in future chapters with many helpful examples given.

Those who worked with alcoholics soon realized, however, that the behavioral pattern of codependency is not restricted to those in relationship with an alcoholic. Melody Beattie was one of the first to make codependence a national buzz-word in her ground-breaking and best-selling book, *Codependent No More: How to Stop Controlling Others and Start Caring For Yourself.*

Before going into descriptions about what codependence *is,* how it works and why it's destructive in relationships, first let me describe what codependence is *not.*

INTERDEPENDENCE

Healthy individuals grow from children who are totally *de*pendent, gradually become *in*dependent as young adults, and finally, ideally, become appropriately *inter*dependent. Interdependence is healthy awareness that we cannot survive alone. For instance, most of us depend on farmers to grow our food, transportation companies to deliver it to our local store, and the store to sell it to us for our consumption. I could cite many other examples of interdependence at work in the culture where most of us live and work.

Another example of interdependence is found in businesses. The president of the company has the vision for the future and negotiates moves toward that goal in order to keep his employees employed and paid. Employees each have their jobs that, together, produce the product that keeps the company prosperous. Neither could do their jobs effectively without the other.

*Inter*dependence is not *co*dependence.

SELECTIVITY

In healthy, functioning households, as well as in most business partnerships, we also practice what is known as selectivity. Selectivity occurs when two persons divide up the chores of daily living according to who does what best. If he does a better job with the laundry, then he takes over laundry chores. If she loves gardening and has a knack for making the yard beautiful, then she may do all or most of the gardening. If neither likes to cook, they may take turns or do the cooking jointly. If one cooks, the other may do the clean-up.

At work, selectivity is seen when two or more persons partner to build a business. My father and his two brothers partnered in a farming business. My dad was the farmer, responsible for growing the crops in sufficient bulk to fill the orders. One of his brothers was responsible for keeping the tractors and trucks running that tilled the fields and delivered the produce to markets. The third brother had a head for business and became the person responsible for paperwork, lease contracts, sales agreements, etc. They successfully functioned as partners because each did what he was best at doing.

Selectivity is characteristic of great partnerships, either at home or at work.

Selectivity is not codependence.

CARE-GIVING
Caring for someone who is, either temporarily or permanently unable to care for himself, is not codependence. Caring for someone who is disabled may be called love, responsibility, friendship or sacrifice but it is not codependence.

EXAMPLES of TEMPORARY CARE-GIVING
My late husband Jim's house burned to the ground in the middle of the night many years ago. The family was lucky that all but their dog escaped alive, Jim wearing only his briefs. As they watched the fire trucks arrive, a neighbor lent him a pair of trousers, and a shirt. Another found a pair of shoes that would work for a few days. As the slow process of insurance claims and rebuilding took place, a friend gave Jim $10,000 as a down payment on another house so they could move out of the motel.

When my niece was diagnosed with breast cancer and began debilitating chemo treatments, her family's friends took turns delivering meals.

Often after a disaster such as a tornado or hurricane, whole communities rally around the survivors bringing clean drinking water, temporary housing, meals and trucks for hauling away debris.

In time, the caregivers were grateful these victims had recovered and allowed them to resume their normal responsibilities. Jim's friend did not continue his gift by making the monthly mortgage payments. As my niece recovered and was physically able, her friends discontinued delivering meals. When a community has been rebuilt, emergency teams move their resources to some other needy community.

My parents were very capable of taking care of themselves until near the end of their lives. In their late eighties, each of them needed physical assistance and emotional support. For my dad, that meant that my sisters and I set up shifts and took turns caring for him during the day. We eventually hired a night nurse to care for him at night and were grateful for the support of our local hospice organization. My mother was not strong enough to meet his needs during this time and greatly appreciated the care-giving roles their daughters assumed until his death.

A few years later, my mother, although largely self-sufficient, needed more nutritious meals and someone to help her safely shower. The three of us who lived closest took turns for several months. Finally we helped her move into a facility that cared for her until her death.

Temporary care-giving is not codependence.

PERMANENT CARE-GIVING

Sometimes caring for babies or young toddlers feels like it will go on forever…will be permanent. But in most cases, children learn to walk so they no longer need to be carried. A growing child even insists on "I can do it myself!" Eventually, children learn skills that enable them to become adults, physically and financially independent. The parents of healthy, independent adult children are fortunate. Some children are born with disabilities that require long-term or lifetime care. Parents of severely disabled children must rise to an elevated level of responsible caretaking that most of us are not required to experience. This may include personally caring for the disabled child. In some cases, it means finding paid or volunteer helpers to assist, or a facility geared to caring for the disabled.

Permanent care-giving, when necessary, is not codependence.

WHERE CARE-GIVING AND CODEPENDENCE INTERSECT

With the on-going reality of war, disabled veterans need partial or total care-giving. Adults who are war-wounded, disabled by an accident, or victims of a catastrophic event such as a stroke, present their caretakers with the need for discernment. How much care-giving is necessary? Too much care-giving can strip away a person's healthy desire to work for a better quality of life. Too little may make the victim feel hopeless...or compromise his or her health. This is a decision point where necessary care-giving and codependence that weakens the will, have to be identified and each handled differently.

When my eldest son Steven was diagnosed with a severely enlarged heart, he returned home to live with Jim and me. He had several medications he needed to take on a regular schedule in order to minimize the stress on his compromised heart. Due to his years of drug addiction and severe Attention Deficit Disorder with Hyperactivity, (ADHD) he found it difficult to do anything according to a schedule. I agonized over the decision of whether or not to take charge of his medicines. On the one hand, it appeared that, most days, he was coping very well, even able to hold down a part-time job. On the other hand, forgetting to take his meds could result in another hospital stay or his premature death. I was told his condition was terminal, but I wanted him to live as long as possible. Walking the tight-rope between necessary assistance and codependence was agonizing. I eventually landed on the side of distributing his meds to him on the recommended schedule. There were other responsibilities that I left in Steven's hands. After two and a half years, no amount of medication could keep his heart going. I'm grateful for the extra time I had with him and do not regret my decision, even though some might label that choice "codependence."

The care-giver must discern between healthful care-giving and unhealthy codependence. This care-giver deserves grace for navigating in a murky area.

SUMMARY
Codependence and the need for setting reasonable boundaries are topics that are not simple, and do not lend themselves to easy formulas. That is why the chapters in this ***Love Potions*** volume will present a variety

of views of codependent characteristics and behaviors, as well as stories of effective, healthy boundary setting.

The examples given above of Interdependence, Selectivity, Temporary and Permanent Care-giving are not to be confused with Codependence. There are situations where only the individuals involved can make an informed choice between healthy, necessary care-giving and unhealthy codependence.

STIR THE POT
As you read this chapter, what relationships came to your mind? Are there situations where you assume responsibility and then resent that the burden falls on you? Are there persons in your life that seem mostly to be on the receiving side of your care and rarely on the giving side? What do you hope to learn from this book?

Chapter 2: SO WHAT IS IT?

Codependence is assuming responsibility for someone else's behavior or feelings. Codependence is doing for others what they are capable of and should be doing for themselves. Codependence is blocking the consequences that someone else should rightfully experience as a result of his or her choices. Codependence is actively or passively supporting an unhealthy or self-destructive behavior in another. Codependence is assuming more than one's share of blame. And more...

Codependence is caused by: low self-esteem, a misunderstanding of love, fear of being thought of as mean or heartless, fear of watching the suffering brought on by another, lack of awareness of one's own feelings and needs, considering another's needs more important than one's own, assuming more than one's share of responsibility, trying to "fix" a situation or another person's life, an imbalance of power or control. And more...

Codependence results in relationships that are messy and unhappy for at least one person, and often both persons. Codependent relationships sometimes create so much distress, distrust, resentment and agony that one or both persons in the relationship just want it to end...and often end the codependence by ending the relationship, only to find another person with whom to have a codependent relationship.

Those who practice codependence usually blame the person with whom they are locked in this unhappy dance. The dance is practiced when the person who is needy is "chosen" by a person who gets some immediate reward from care-taking or rescuing. Codependents find (or create) relationships where the other person is needy, helpless, or irresponsible. Codependents often feel pity for the person with whom they are locked in this dysfunctional dance. Decisions are made out of pity and fear, rather than from love. (More about this later!) And then the blaming begins.

Gay and Kathlyn Hendricks in their book, *Conscious Loving: The Journey to Co-Commitment,* summarize codependence very well. "Codependence is fostered when two people unconsciously agree to be the partners in each other's dramas. An unconscious bargain is stuck: If you won't make me change my self-destructive patterns, I won't make you change yours. If you will let me project my childhood issues onto you, I'll be the target for yours. The trouble is that codependence feels so bad that people start complaining shortly after the dramas get under way. At that point, we start to blame our troubles on the other person."

Dr. Phil Magraw of radio, TV and book fame, frequently states that, "We train others how to treat us." Codependents do this very effectively. Codependents train others to treat them with disrespect, or unconsciously reward manipulation or inappropriate dependence. A codependent seems to invite others to take advantage of him or to disregard her needs. A codependent may positively reward manipulation, encourage unnecessary helplessness and assume the burden of unpleasant consequences created by another, and more…

We are each capable of being on both sides of the codependent dance. I may be the codependent rescuer at one time, or in one relationship, and then be the manipulative, needy user at another time, or in another relationship. This book will focus primarily on the codependent person's behaviors and recovery, however. It is usually the codependent who must establish boundaries in order to free oneself, and often the other, from this destructive pattern of relationship.

PERSONAL EXAMPLE

Much of what I share comes from the painful experiences of being a dedicated codependent. I still find myself falling into subtle codependent behaviors or discovering codependent patterns or beliefs so deeply embedded that it's taken years of learning and living for them to surface. I forgive myself for the length of the journey, and am grateful for the liberation that comes each time I recognize and disconnect from codependent entrapments. But then, without all those painful lessons in codependence, I wouldn't have anything useful to say in this book.

About the time I experienced the eye-opening lesson with the carpenter recounted in the preview of this book, my son Steve was in the fourth grade. In California, all fourth graders learn about the missions founded by Father Serra along the entire coastline. These missions include San Juan Capistrano (famous for the swallows that return each year to nest), Santa Barbara, San Francisco, and eighteen others.

Steve's teacher gave the students an assignment to build a small model of one of the missions using any materials they wanted, including paper, cardboard, popsicle sticks, etc. This assignment was given several weeks ahead of its due date. The first time I heard about this assignment was when Steve told me about it the night before it was due.

I exploded. Why hadn't I heard about this before? Why hadn't he gotten started on it? Did the teacher send a notice home that I didn't receive?

When I calmed down, we hopped in the car, drove through McDonalds for a quick dinner, went to the craft store for supplies and got to work. It didn't even occur to me that he would benefit from suffering the consequences of turning in the assignment late. If I had stopped to think it through, I might have realized that I was operating out of my own ego...pride that my child would do as well in school as I did, be as responsible as I was, perform well. But at that time, I wasn't that conscious.

Instead, I sat with him, listened to his ideas, and then, together, we built a model of a mission. We finished about 11 p.m. that night. He turned it in on time. I believe he got an A for our efforts. But what had I taught him? What had he learned?

One night when he was fifteen years old, he sneaked his step-sister's Mustang keys out of her purse and went joy riding. Until 2 a.m. when a policeman knocked on the door, I thought Steve was home, asleep. He was in jail. Again, I rescued him, placing a $12,000 lien on our house in order to bail him out. While writing this, I had to ask my step-daughter if Steve paid for the damage done to her car (yes) and did he pay for the ticket (yes). I know the lien was removed from the house so he must have shown up in court when required, probably with me as his escort. My newly acquired step-daughter felt justifiably violated. She asked for, and received, permission to put a lock on her door. I remember feeling horrified that my son would do such a thing!

By the time he was seventeen years old, he had a Camaro carcass parked in the back yard that he'd cannibalized for parts to put a working Camaro together. I frequently nagged him about getting rid of the rusting hulk. He promised. Over and over again, he promised. But nothing happened.

Finally, thinking of the lesson with the carpenter, I asked Steve, "When is the earliest you can get the car hauled away?" He answered, "Next Sunday." I replied, "O.K. If it isn't gone by 3 p.m. I'll call someone to haul it to a junk yard for scrap." He agreed. I quit nagging.

Sunday came. About 1 p.m., as he was leaving for a friend's house, he said to me, "I can't get to it today, but I'll take care of it tomorrow." I quietly replied, "That's not our deal. Our deal was that it'd be gone by 3 p.m. today. If it isn't, I'm calling someone to haul it away."

Steve was angry. I was calm. He called a friend who had a trailer, borrowed it, and by 3 p.m. our yard no longer looked like the local junk heap!

There's a lot of back-story in regard to the journey Steven and I took together. Although he was young when it happened, his father's death deeply affected him. In his twenties, I began hearing about ADHD

(Attention Deficit Disorder with Hyperactivity) and realized that, from infancy, Steve had all the symptoms, but had never been diagnosed. There was a growing body of research linking ADHD with a predilection for drug abuse. He was constantly frustrated with the gap between his enormously high intelligence and giftedness with math and mechanical things, and his inability to follow through. And then there was my codependent, rescuing beliefs and behaviors that contributed to his patterns of behavior.

I gradually learned about, and slowly disconnected from my codependent ways that, in the early years, supported his addictive patterns. In his late twenties, Steve's ADHD symptoms improved after a series of bio-feedback sessions at the Drake Institute in Los Angeles, but it was too late to save him from the effects of his drug addiction. Steven's very determined life choices eventually resulted in his death from congestive heart failure.

I consider Steven one of my most profound and valuable life-teachers. I have no doubt that he, with all of his glorious, joyous gifts, as well as his enormously frustrating choices, was given to me, and I to him. I believe that there are no mistakes…only life-lessons that are perfectly designed for whatever we are sent here to learn. Steven gave me a great deal of joy, loved me unconditionally, believed in me, *and* was the source of many crises that pushed me to the edge of sanity until the lessons were learned.

I am absolutely sure that I have his blessing in sharing some of the lessons I learned from being his mother. At another time, in another volume, I hope to share more about this precious soul and our journey together. But in *this* volume, you'll hear more about the lessons learned in relationship to him about codependency and boundaries.

As I became more conscious of the effects of my choices, I became able to more frequently make decisions in all of my relationships from a foundation of love, not pity or fear. Choices made from authentic love are *always* healthier and more empowering to both parties. Choices made out of pity or fear, inevitably weaken or damage both persons and the relationship between them.

SUMMARY

Codependency is a complex mix of beliefs, relationship patterns, emotions and behaviors that is impossible to wrap up in a tidy little box. There is no doubt that codependent behaviors create difficulties in relationships that cause a great deal of pain. Because it's painful, codependent persons frequently blame the person with whom they are in relationship rather than identifying and changing the choices that keep them locked in this dysfunctional pattern. A codependent teaches others to depend on him or her in ways that are manipulative and disempowering to both persons in the relationship. The goal of recovery is to make relationship choices that are empowering to both parties.

STIR THE POT

Did any of the descriptions of codependency in this chapter remind you of your own behaviors? How did you feel as you read the story about Steven and his fourth grade project? Do you relate to my struggles with a teenager who was out of control? What other painful relationships came to mind as you read this chapter?

Chapter 3: AM I CODEPENDENT?

There are many descriptions of codependent behavior and/or the results from a pattern of codependency in a relationship. One of the simplest, and therefore the definition of codependency that I rely on, is "An imbalance of responsibility." In a relationship, that means that one person assumes too much responsibility, while the other person assumes too little. And you might be overly responsible in one area or in one relationship and not carrying your share of the load in another area, or relationship.

The following description is from www.wikihow.com/tell-if-you-are-codependent: "Underdeveloped self-esteem combined with an inappropriate caring for others and an inappropriate reliance on another's response in a negatively reinforcing loop." In plainer language that means that I (1) allow others to walk all over me at times, and other times (2) invade another's business without being invited and (3) depend on others' approval of me in order to feel good about myself. These three patterns tend to cycle through a codependent's life over and over again.

In her book, *Codependency for Dummies*, Licensed Marriage and Family Therapist Darlene Lancer says that if you were raised in a dysfunctional family or had an ill parent, you're likely codependent. That precursor may include many of us! Ms. Lancer describes the symptoms of codependency rather than trying to define it. Here's her list: (Italics are mine.)

Low Self-esteem – Feeling that you're not good enough, or comparing yourself to others while always coming out "less than." He may appear to feel good about himself, but it's only a disguise. He may actually believe he's unlovable, or underneath she feels shame because she isn't good enough. *Perfectionism and codependence often go hand in hand.*

People-pleasing – There's nothing wrong with wanting to please someone for whom you care, but codependents believe they have no choice. *Saying "no" causes unreasonable anxiety.* Codependents often sacrifice their own needs to accommodate the desires of others.

Poor boundaries – A boundary is an imaginary line between you and another. It applies to property including your body, money, belongings, but also applies to your feelings, thoughts and needs. *Codependents often feel responsible for another person's feelings and problems or blame their own on someone else.* Sometimes people flip back and forth between having weak boundaries and having rigid ones that close them off from healthy relationships.

Reactivity – A consequence of poor boundaries is that you over react to others' thoughts and feelings. You either believe what is said or become defensive. *You absorb another's critical words, feeling the sting deep within.* With a boundary, you'd be more evaluative, realizing it was just his or her opinion, and not be as threatened by disagreements.

Caretaking – If someone else has a problem, you want to help them to the point that you give up yourself, your needs, your feelings. It's way beyond empathy. Empathy means feeling what another feels, imagining what it may be like for that person. Codependents step into the other's circumstances and feelings and want to *spend their energy trying to fix* *the other person*, even when the other may not have asked for it and isn't taking the codependent's advice.

Control – Having control helps codependents feel safe and secure. Everyone needs some control. None of us wants to live in constant uncertainty and chaos. But for codependents, control limits his ability to take risks or share her feelings. Sometimes an addiction to alcohol or drugs is an aid to helping a codependent let go of control, or *manage the feelings of being out of control.* Codependents also need to control those close to them in order for the codependent to feel okay. *Codependents may be perceived as bossy.*

Dysfunctional communication – Codependents have trouble communicating their thoughts, feelings, and needs. Often it's because a codependent doesn't know what he thinks or feels or needs. Other times, she knows, but won't be truthful for fear of upsetting someone. *Communication is dishonest and confusing* when one tries to manipulate the other person out of fear.

Obsessions – Codependents have a tendency to obsess about other people, situations or relationships. *This obsessing is a symptom of dependency, anxiety and fear.* A codependent will obsess if she thinks she's made a mistake—did the "wrong" thing or upset someone. He may obsess about the past, or the future to avoid dealing with the here and now.

Dependency – *Codependents need other people to like them in order to feel good about themselves.* He's afraid of being rejected or abandoned. She needs to be in a relationship because she's depressed when on her own. These dependencies make it hard to leave a relationship that is painful or abusive, and so he/she feels trapped.

Denial – Codependents characteristically believe that their problems are the fault of someone else, so *tend to remain in denial about how they are creating their own reality.* The codependent's energy is spent trying to fix the other person or wallowing in self-pity and complaints. Although some codependents seem needy, others act as if they're self-sufficient when it comes to needing help. He has trouble asking for help. She has trouble receiving.

Problems with intimacy – Although this does not necessarily mean a sexual problem (it may be), it is more often an emotional fear of being open and close with someone. Because of shame and weak boundaries, you might *fear that you'll be judged, rejected, or left. Or you may fear being smothered and losing your autonomy, denying your need for closeness.*

Painful emotions – *Codependency creates stress and leads to painful emotions.* Shame and low self-esteem create anxiety and fear about being judged, rejected, making mistakes, being a failure, feeling trapped by being too close, or being alone. When the feelings become overwhelming, you may seek help, recovery and change. One free resource is the support group called Codependents Anonymous. And, of course, reading a book like this one may open many doors of discovery and ideas for better ways of handling your emotions and relationships.

DON'T PANIC
As I went through this list, I realized that nearly every descriptive statement was true of me at one time and in some degree or another. I still am very prone to codependent tendencies and have to guard against falling into the familiar emotional traps that have swallowed me in the past.

According to research, *left untreated, or unacknowledged, the symptoms of codependency tend to become worse.* But just as any habit that does not support ones' health can be changed, codependency is a pattern of beliefs and behaviors that can be changed. These patterns were once learned. They can be unlearned. Healthier beliefs and behaviors can be substituted for previously codependent ones. As with changing any habit, this substitution of healthy for unhealthy will be a process that takes place over time. Fortunately, our lives—family, work, and relationships—provide plenty of opportunities to practice.

A dedicated codependent's reaction to this list of symptoms may be extreme. She may think, "I've been doing things all wrong. It's all my fault. I need to fix this now!" He may think, "No wonder I've had one failed relationship after another. I'm going to just be manly about this, and from now on, I won't need anyone! I can take care of myself."

Stop right there! Let me describe what is a healthier response to this news so you can begin to practice non-codependent thinking right now! A more balanced response is, "I'm realizing something about myself that I want to change. I'm going to adopt an attitude of curiosity. I'll just watch what happens within my relationships and how I react. I'll ask myself questions that are caring—exploratory—not judgmental or shaming. I'll begin by just noticing what is. I'll keep reading and learning. And in the spirit of experiment, I'll try on some new thoughts, ideas, beliefs and behaviors and see how they feel. I'm going to be kind to myself as I go through this exploration and carefully choose new behaviors or attitudes as I am ready."

Beneficial change does not occur as a result of shaming. Positive change occurs most easily when surrounded by kindness, reinforcement and patience. These are gifts you can begin giving yourself today...and continue giving each and every day of your life. You will not "spoil" yourself. Perhaps the first belief that needs to be exchanged for a healthier one is that "beating myself up is the only way to get better." The truth is that beating ourselves up only keeps us stuck where we are, reinforcing the very thing we wish to change. Change occurs most easily in an atmosphere of compassionate acceptance. After years of working to disconnect myself from codependency, as well as making other changes in my life, I still have to remind myself of this gentle truth every day.

SUMMARY
Codependency is a subject that, although it has one title, has many different ways of being experienced. Some characteristics may apply to you. Other may not apply to you. Reading a concentrated, potent list of symptoms as described in this chapter may feel overwhelming to some. Try to just notice your internal reaction...what the voice inside your head is saying to you. Notice, but do not emotionally "jump off the cliff." Try reading the quote to yourself from the paragraph beginning "Stop right there!" How does it feel to be kind and gentle with yourself while you explore this topic? Change...recovery...will happen much faster and easier when cradled in compassion.

STIR THE POT: Identifying Codependency

Gently ask yourself "What descriptions in this chapter stood out as probably applying to me? Is it hard for me to identify what I feel? What I want? What I need? Do I notice myself giving in to someone else even when it means great inconvenience to myself? Am I aware that I sometimes allow others to disregard my feelings or needs? Or, are there times I disregard the needs of others in order to get what I want? Am I ready to *kindly* make a change?

A wonderful little book that teaches the power of being kind to yourself is *The Power of Kindness: Change Your Life with Love & Compassion*, by Sharon Salzberg.

Chapter 4: VELCRO

Velcro is used to fasten jogging shoes, wristwatches, windbreakers and even pillow covers. It's that bristly stuff that has loops on one side and tiny little hooks on the other. When they get anywhere near each other the hooks grab the loops and hang on. When you pull them apart it makes a tearing sound, as though fabric was being ripped.

Velcro is a wonderful metaphor for how a codependent relationship works. Just as there are two distinctly different strips that, together, form Velcro, the "co" in codependency refers to the truth that it takes *two* participants for a codependent relationship to exist. Both persons are irresponsible in different ways. "Dependence" refers to each person depending on the other for the things described in the next few paragraphs. The whole relationship doesn't necessarily have to be codependent. There may be areas of the relationship that work very well and other areas that don't.

Two distinct kinds of behavior, one with hooks and the other with loops, come together for the codependent dance to occur. On one side of the relationship, a person will act irresponsibly. From now on I'll call him "Irry," short for "irresponsible." I'm making Irry a "he" for the sake of simplicity. Irry may be either male or female.

He will, perhaps, be late for work, refuse to balance his checkbook or pay his bills on time, thoughtlessly leave messes, procrastinate with projects, blame others for his feelings, or practice an addiction to alcohol, drugs, gambling, raging, sex, work or spending. In areas where he is irresponsible, he treats his dance partner with disrespect, disdain, or blithe indifference and demonstrates thoughtless disregard for the consequences of his choices.

Irry is often charming, masterfully enlisting others to clean up his messes. Or, Irry may be pitiful, enlisting sympathetic assistance. Most of the time, whether by being charming or pitiful, someone agrees to pick up the slack. Although the procrastination was his, the secretary will work overtime preparing his presentation to important clients. A parent will bail him out of legal or financial problems. In spite of his poor credit history, credit card companies continue issuing credit to him. His dance partner may nag or complain, but, nevertheless, will pick up his dirty laundry and used dishes, assume primary responsibility for the parenting of his children, all while forgiving, or at least tolerating his thoughtlessness, neglect or cruelty.

One who assumes Irry's responsibilities or rescues him from unpleasant consequences is called an "enabler." For ease of this narrative, I'll call her Abby, short for "enabler." I'm referring to Abby as a "she" although this role, as well, may be assumed by either gender. Sometimes these roles are traded back and forth in the same relationship.

Irry *depends* on Abby to intercept the uncomfortable consequences that would otherwise be the natural result of his irresponsibility. Irry is also *depending* on Abby to keep him unconscious of his dysfunctional life. As long as there is an Abby around, he needn't face all the ways his life isn't working very well. He may ignore the consequences of drug or alcohol addiction until his body or his life falls apart. He may pretend his addiction to pornography, gambling, or excessive spending, isn't hurting anyone—it's just a little fun in his life. Irry may delude himself into believing that his long hours at work are because the job demands it, or he needs the money or promotion "for his family." As long as Abby tolerates his irresponsibility, lack of good balance, negligent, demeaning behavior, or physical abuse toward her, she supports his belief that, "It's for her own good," or, "This is just the way I am," or, "I can't change," or even, "You're the problem, not me!" Irry usually *depends* on a whole cadre of Abbys to keep him unconscious of his irresponsibility, support his otherwise unbalanced life, and provide someone to blame when he is unhappy.

Abby is also unconsciously *depending* on Irry for some very vital things, as well. She *depends* on him to give her life a sense of purpose. Her purpose is to love him, which really means "save" him by patiently forgiving his faults and cleaning up the messes he leaves in his wake. Often she experiences a self-satisfied righteousness as she "helps" him. If she is successful in making *his* life run smoothly, then *her* life has meaning. She feels important. Abby is *dependent* on her success as his rescuer to convince herself that she is a good person, deserving of love. Deep in her heart she believes that in exchange for all the sacrificial things she does for him, she will be loved. It may take a long time for Abby to wake up to the reality that he didn't agree to that exchange. She will never feel loved in the role of enabler.

In addition, she is *depending* on his dramas to keep her distracted from her own low self-esteem. As long as her energy and attention are used for saving *his* life, she can justify neglecting the work she needs to do in order to take care of *her* life. If she is focused on providing what *he* needs, she is exempt from the hard work of figuring out and getting what *she* needs.

It should come as no surprise that Abby often feels exhausted, overwhelmed and resentful. She also feels ashamed, guilty, and disillusioned. Abby feels ashamed because at some level she knows she is compromising her own integrity, and, at times, hurting others or even breaking the law in order to protect Irry. The level of dishonesty may be profound as she attempts to convince herself she is happy and loves him, while Irry's behavior continues to drain her of self-respect. She feels guilty, because no matter how much she does for him, she is failing to make him happy or his life good. She is disillusioned, because she thought "saving" him would make her life meaningful, but instead, it feels wasted. As codependency runs its course, Abby feels hopelessness, despair, and profound bitterness. In essence, Abby has abdicated responsibility for her own life, feelings, and welfare. Codependency, therefore, is a disease of mutual, interlocking irresponsibility.

There may be genuine love at the heart of the relationship between Irry and Abby. The mixture of love and self-deception is what makes codependency so hard to separate from reasonable helping and healthy support.

THE RESULT

The two persons who make up a codependent relationship find each other like the hooks and loops of Velcro. They stick. They fit. Each partner practices patterns of behavior that strengthen and support the dysfunctional beliefs and behaviors of the other. They end up feeling trapped and resent, or eventually even hate each other for the dance they co-create. Irry is angry because Abby didn't "fix" him and Abby is enraged because all of her inner resources have been used up without receiving the love she thought would be the reward. In the long view, neither person gets what is really needed.

As long as they both believe that this is how their needs will be met, however, they have very compelling reasons for keeping this "Velcro" arrangement going. Both persons remain stuck in patterns that make it easy to blame the other for his or her unhappy life. As long as Irry can blame Abby for not helping him enough, or letting him down when he really needed her, or keeping his life miserable with her unhappiness and demands for change, he can avoid the painful awareness of his own culpability. He sees himself as Abby's victim rather than looking at his lack of self-responsibility. As long as Abby can blame Irry's neediness, negligence or abuse for her unhappy, unfulfilled life, she doesn't have to look at her voluntary participation in the relationship. She sees herself as his victim rather than acknowledging that she has abandoned her life to the control of another.

Inevitably, codependency begets blame. With blame, the solution to unhappiness remains "out there" in the hands of another person or a change in circumstances. This point of view keeps one perpetually a victim of things beyond his or her control. Blame, resentment, depression, guilt, shame and defensiveness are just a *few* of the results of this pattern.

Over the years, I have identified myself as both Irry and Abby at different times—in the same relationship or in different relationships.

A CODEPENDENT FRIENDSHIP

I once had a friendship with Jill. At the beginning of the relationship, I was Irry. I was widowed at the age of twenty-three. I met Jill soon afterward. I was still trying to recover some balance. Jill and her husband were so kind, warmly welcoming the boys and me into their lives. We spent a great deal of time with them. In hindsight, I believe I handed them a big chunk of the responsibility for helping me to heal and for sharing some of the heavy responsibility for two little boys. Jill, in particular, rearranged her life around our needs, and I willingly accepted the huge commitment of time and energy she gave to us.

Years went by. I became stronger. I was ready to assume more responsibility for my life. I began to venture out from the protective umbrella of Jill's friendship. I didn't want to lose her as a friend, but I wanted more friends. I also wanted to find a man with whom I could share my life; but whenever I had any contact with someone new, or enjoyed an event without her along, she was threatened and suspicious. She would demand all the details. Who did I talk with? Where did I go?

I began to get frequent lectures about how I was letting her down. She had been a friend to me when I needed her, and now I wasn't being a friend to her. I believed her. I had switched roles and was now Abby. I wanted to be a good friend, so I kept trying harder—and feeling more resentful. After a few dates with a man for whom I cared, the whole issue blew up. She wanted me to stop dating him. She didn't think he was right for me. She didn't trust him. I was caught between trying to be a good friend and wanting to move forward with my life. I eventually consulted a counselor for some perspective, because I was so afraid I *really was* a bad friend.

As a result of the counsel given, I decided to ask Jill for some time off from our friendship—time to regain our balance as individuals. I know my request was devastating for her. It hurt me to know how much I was hurting her. Our friendship never recovered. I accept full responsibility for the codependent, Velcro-like roles I played that kept us locked together in a way that was ultimately, devastatingly hurtful to all of us. It was a very painful lesson.

CODEPENDENCY IN MY FAMILY

When I ranted and raved at Jim or the children, I was Irry. I was unconsciously asking them to suffer the consequences of my irresponsible anger. I wanted them to act certain ways, do certain things, treat me a certain way so that I would feel loved, successful—a good wife and mother. When they didn't do what I wanted, I blamed them for my unhappiness. While justifying my behavior as being "for their own good," I was really asking *them* to be responsible for convincing *me* that I was successful as a wife and mother.

While periodically exploding at Jim or the kids, I was also demanding super-human efforts from myself in this quest for the perfect life, perfect family. Something had to give. I became so depressed I could barely get out of bed. I developed insomnia. I began binge eating in secret. I gained a lot of weight. I found a counselor who specialized in eating disorders. Fortunately for me, she understood the root cause to be a combination of over-responsibility for others in an attempt to win love, coupled with under-responsibility for my own welfare. The conflict had created a volcano of such frightening feelings that I had driven them underground. Those powerful feelings had erupted as an eating disorder.

Denying or being unaware of one's feelings is one of the common symptoms of codependency. Codependents seem to have an overdeveloped sixth sense about the feelings of others, but have a lot of difficulty identifying their own feelings or allowing themselves to feel their own feelings.

I was encouraged to journal as a safe outlet for my feelings. In addition, she gave me permission to ease up on my excessive responsibilities for others, while learning to be more responsible for myself. At first, I couldn't believe that recovery could come by being *less* responsible! I was terrified! Wouldn't I disappoint or even damage those I loved if I backed away from taking care of them? "Them" included Jim, the kids, the boss, the business, the house, the parents, et al. Mightn't our lives just crumble if I didn't keep everything running? I believed that I needed to sacrifice myself in order for the needs of those I loved to be met, and in order for me to be loved. I was afraid that if I made decisions in support of my own well-being, someone I loved would be neglected . . . or possibly the world would end!

ASSIGNMENT: BE IRRESPONSIBLE?

I began to look for a situation where I could experiment with being a *little* irresponsible without hurting anyone, just for practice. I wanted to break the strangle-hold that "being responsible" had on me. Two weeks later, I was buying groceries. I picked up a carton of yogurt, and somehow, between the shelf and my cart, it slipped out of my hand. Splat! The lid flew off and blueberry yogurt spread out in a three-foot wide star-burst pattern! I stood there looking at it for a minute, then burst out laughing, and walked away! I just walked away! How irresponsible!

I knew someone would report it to the manager, but this time, it wouldn't be me! Someone would be paid to clean it up. It didn't have to be me! Accidents happen. I decided not to grovel in apology to the manager repeating "I'm sorry" over and over or grabbing a mop and cleaning it up myself. I walked up and down the aisles, finishing my shopping, with a grin from ear to ear. I must have looked a little ditzy. I didn't care! It was a giant step for me to take. I felt liberated! I didn't have to hold the whole world together by my excessive sense of responsibility. That silly escapade gave me hope.

Gradually, I learned to let go of responsibilities that weren't really mine and relaxed my grip on the consuming fear of being imperfect. I still remember the sensation of an enormous weight lifting off of me when I was told that just because there was a job that needed doing, I didn't have to do it. And even if I could do a particular job better than someone else, I *still* didn't have to do it! I began to love myself rather than attempting the impossible task of *earning* love. Slowly, I became more responsible for *myself.*

DIAGNOSTIC ASSISTANCE

Melody Beattie said that we take care of people's responsibilities for them. Later we get mad at *them* for what *we've* done. Then we feel used and sorry for ourselves. That is the pattern, the triangle. This list of a few characteristics of codependency was extracted from a much more comprehensive list in *Co-dependent No More* by Melody Beattie:

"Doing something we really don't want to do. Saying 'yes' when we mean 'no.' Doing something for someone although that person is capable of and should be doing it for him or herself. Meeting people's needs without being asked and before we've agreed to do so. Consistently giving more than we receive in a particular situation. Trying to fix another's feelings. (Doing something *just* to make them feel better.) Doing another person's job for them. Speaking for another person. Solving people's problems for them. Putting more interest and activity into a joint effort than the other person does. Not asking for what we want, need and desire."

SUMMARY

Separating two persons from their unconscious contracts that support mutual irresponsibility results in a tearing apart that is often noisy, just like separating strips of Velcro. It rarely happens quietly. It's a new beginning, the birth of a healthier life—messy and painful—but a necessary step to the freedom of healthier relationships.

STIR THE POT: Disconnecting Velcro Strips

What did you relate to as you read this chapter? What questions are coming to mind? Does the idea of loosening the bonds of responsibility strike terror in your heart? In what relationships or circumstances do you experience resentment? What are you doing that you don't want to do? Where are you saying "yes" when you really want is to say "no." What is keeping you from saying "no?" What are you afraid of? Who are you afraid of losing? How would it feel to take care of *yourself*? What is one step, one thing, you can do today that would be self-nurturing? (For instance: take a bubble bath, set aside 30 minutes to read something you enjoy, begin writing your thoughts and feelings down in a journal, make a lunch date with a friend, take a walk after dinner, join a community sports team, etc.) Will you do it?

Chapter 5: THE INVISIBLE BARRIER

S o turn the kaleidoscope a bit and let's view the pieces of codependency in a slightly different pattern…

As described in the previous chapter, two persons in a codependent pattern are stuck together like the hooks and loops of Velcro. While joined in this crazy-making dance, they are also separated by a barrier erected from the blocks of unhappy feelings created by codependence. Both analogies are helpful in understanding codependence. Resentment, blame, guilt, crippling pity and shame are a few of the blocks that build the invisible barrier. Those feelings prevent the possibility of a healthy, fully loving relationship.

Just as a wall is built one block at a time, a dysfunctional, codependent relationship develops with the use of one disrespectful response, one irresponsible or enabling act, one limiting belief at a time. As individual responsibilities, fears and resentments are not dealt with in a healthy, respectful way, the wall grows thicker and higher. The cement gluing the blocks together into a wall is a misunderstanding of love. We'll look more closely at that misunderstanding in the next chapter.

In this chapter, the anagram of BARRIER will help describe the characteristics and results of codependence in a relationship. Just as with the communication tools taught in **Communication Elixirs**, if healthy boundaries of responsibility were not demonstrated in my home of origin, then the *concept must be understood* before healthy responsibility can be *practiced*.

Boundaries between responsibilities are blurred

Where there are fences between our house and the houses on either side of us, it is easy to distinguish between the property that is ours to maintain, and the property that is the responsibility of our neighbors. In contrast, the boundaries between individuals' responsibilities are much harder to define.

As a healthy adult, the things for which I must be responsible, remain in my "yard" so to speak. In a healthy *relationship*, the things for which the other person must be responsible remain in the other person's yard. It's as though we each have an invisible property line surrounding us within which we "own" our individual stuff . . . stuff for which no one else can be *appropriately* responsible.

There are some things that even a great partner, friend or relative cannot do for me. No one else can, with good results, take care of my job, my role as a spouse or parent, or assume the burden of the consequences when I am irresponsible. No partner can successfully *make* me happy, or *make* my life meaningful, or *make* me feel loved. All of those outcomes remain in *my* yard.

Another may, if he or she chooses, contribute to all of those things—by being supportive, by participating in a mutually honoring relationship of personal growth, by being flexible about life changes, by loving me in meaningful ways. All of which means that I, too, may give support, honor, flexibility and love.

When I step over into another's yard, assuming responsibilities or consequences that can only, with healthy results, be assumed by him or her, the vicious dogs of resentment, defensiveness, blame, and crippling irresponsibility soon attack me. At the same time, the dogs in *my* yard are complaining because they aren't being fed. Each time the boundary of appropriate responsibility is crossed, a block is placed between us erecting a barrier to a healthy relationship.

There are boundaries that *encircle each relationship,* as well, delineating a healthy separation between it and all other relationships. In a marriage, for example, the boundary of emotional and sexual faithfulness is the most foundational. The deepest experience of romantic love cannot be experienced when one or both partners dilutes the quality of their commitment or love by sharing it outside the marriage with fantasy, pornography, adultery or other active addictions. The relationship is compromised when one partner has relationships or activities that take precedence over the needs of the marriage or marriage partner, robbing the marriage of the energy and intimacy that it needs for good health.

In other relationships, as well as in marriage, the boundaries of loyalty and truthfulness apply. Sharing confidences told you by your best friend is a violation of loyalty. Sharing trade secrets belonging to your employer is punishable by law.

Every relationship has its own boundaries that are designed to help it flourish. When healthy relationship boundaries are maintained, the individuals in that relationship are also protected.

ADDICTION TO CONTROL AND APPROVAL

There seems to be a see-saw-like cycle to codependency. One cycle is *control.* I must have the house exactly so. I demand to know where you are every minute and exactly what time you'll be home. I must be sure you are not practicing an addiction. I must have you with me at all times. I must have all facets of any particular part of my life aligned just the way I want them or I'll make you pay—either by a foul mood, silence, criticism, judgment, raging, or more extreme abuse.

An obsessive compulsion to force someone else to do what I want him to do or be what I want him to be—to fit into the mold I've constructed for him—is an addiction to control, one of the symptoms of codependency. This may take the form of excessive worry and/or nagging. Another characteristic of an addiction to control is that I expend more energy trying to force the *other* person to change than I spend on examining how *I* need to change. I spend more time in *his* yard than in my own!

The corresponding cycle is the need for *approval*. I will do anything to please you. I will put myself through Houdini contortions to make sure that you are happy with me . . . approve of me . . . love me. The obsessive need for approval keeps me chasing after the one whose approval I crave. Usually, with the characteristic wisdom of the universe, the one being pursued continues backing away or withholding his or her approval. It is clear that the unhealthy craving for another's approval will never bring the self-worth or love I crave.

The two halves of the cycle are saying something like, "You're not doing it right. I'll do it!" and then "I have to sacrifice myself, doing things I resent doing, in order to have your approval."

One wife in a workshop shared that she wants the house cleaned a particular way. She wants her husband to help her, but when he doesn't do it up to her standards, she is resentful. She says something like, "Oh, just forget it! I'll do it myself!" Of course her husband was less and less enthusiastic about helping since he can never please her. She realized her need to control the miniscule differences between her way and his way was damaging their relationship. She must decide between doing it her way, happily and alone, or sharing the load without a rigid need for control.

A friend of mine is a whiz at getting things done, and done very well. In the office where she works, she has a pattern of assuming new responsibilities without relinquishing any of her current tasks. She is exhausted and often resentful because her life is out of balance. She sacrifices her energy and spare time trying to win approval and control the quality of work. Gradually she is learning to re-claim a more reasonable balance between her contributions at work and reasonable self-care.

RESISTANCE TO FEELINGS

A classic symptom of codependency is resistance to feelings. While enabling the irresponsibility of another, I resist admitting that I feel resentful. I try to "make" myself feel happy to give. I shush my internal whispers of dissatisfaction. I shove down my anger. I hide being upset because I don't want to hurt someone. I tell myself, "I shouldn't feel this way." I make excuses for not dealing with my feelings by saying things like, "He (she) *needs* me," or "I can't change things, so why try," or "A *good* person would be patient, loving, encouraging."

While acting irresponsibly toward my own needs, I resist the feelings of shame. I defend myself and blame others for my failures. I live on the shallow surface of my feelings, reluctant to examine the low self-worth that is at my core when I neglect responsibilities that are really mine. I shove all hints of my own longing for self-respect far below the surface of my awareness.

I'm also resistant to the other's feelings. I am overly concerned about being the object of the other's displeasure or of hurting his or her feelings. I'm afraid to speak up when I feel hurt or disappointed, so I "stuff" it in order to *protect* the other. A healthy relationship is built on truth, not pretending.

I am resistant to feelings if, when my friend is unhappy, I try to make him or her cheer up. I may move heaven and earth to help a loved one, and then feel angry when my efforts aren't appreciated.

All of these feelings are hints that something essential to my wellbeing is being ignored.

I was picking up a prescription in the drug store. Several people were waiting in line. A little boy scratched his leg on the edge of the display and began to cry. His grandmother held her hand over his mouth whispering, "Shhhh!" over and over. She was resistant to his very normal expression of pain, and uncomfortable with the attention that was focused on them.

Through death, I have lost two husbands and a child. I have heard all of the things people say to the bereaved in an effort to make them stop hurting. Why isn't it O.K. to just hurt? To grieve? Why do so many want the survivor to hurry up and feel better? Perhaps because he is resistant to the feelings that come with grieving a loss and the long process involved in recovery from a great loss. Perhaps she is resisting awareness that loss may happen to her, as well.

My late husband Jim conducted a funeral service for a man who had been the widow's husband for 55 years. Her son escorted her up to the open coffin after the service to say "good-bye." The old woman began to cry softly. The son said, "Now, Mother! You've done real good. Don't let me down now!" He was so resistant to feelings that he couldn't let his mother grieve the death of the man with whom she had shared her life for 55 years!

RESCUE OTHERS FROM CONSEQUENCES

It's appropriate to rescue a child from the consequences of running into a busy street. It is not appropriate to buy booze for an alcoholic, or bail out a repeat offender, or lend money to someone who foolishly squandered the rent money, or lie to an employer to cover another's "sick day" spent fishing, or take back home an abusive spouse who has not consented to therapy or demonstrated emotional stability, or make up excuses for a spouse who has missed an important occasion with a child, or protect another from disappointment when I say, "no." Every time I step in-between a capable person's action and its natural consequence I am interfering with his or her opportunity to learn.

When my son Steven was an adult, we once discussed my practice of rescuing him from the consequences of his behavior. He told me that, at an early age, he learned (remember the California Missions Project?) that if he just endured my initial anger, I would eventually jump into the situation and fix it for him. That was not my intention, but my consistent rescuing reinforced an expectation and behavior pattern in Steve that did not serve him very well.

I met with a couple several times before their wedding. In the past, she had caught him in a couple of relatively minor lies, things he passed off as jokes or inconsequential. Then it leaked out that while on a business trip he'd stopped in to see his old girlfriend, although he'd assured his fiancée that he hadn't. This soon-to-be-bride had been hesitant about the previous incidents, but this time the lie could not possibly fall into the "joke" or "inconsequential" categories. I'm convinced that he never assumed responsibility for the lie or the consequence of her loss of trust. She wanted the marriage so badly that, in my opinion, she eventually glossed over the issue. If, indeed, she did do that, she left the door open for future lies and further loss of trust—more blocks stacked in the Invisible Barrier.

A complicating dilemma arises when the consequences of another's choices cause suffering for you and, perhaps, your children. If his or her behavior results in the rent not being paid, for instance, the stakes are high and the choices much more difficult. It takes amazing balance to find a way through such a tangle of difficult emotions and options. During a time like this, faith is the only place I know of to find refuge and wisdom. It may be faith in God, faith in the support of the universe, faith in yourself, or faith in the tenets of a support group such as Codependents Anonymous, but faith is needed to rip apart the Velcro to gain freedom from the prison of codependency. (Codependents Anonymous is a nation-wide support group listed in most local directories.)

INEQUALITY OR INAPPROPRIATE INVOLVEMENT

Codependency is such a complex mix of behaviors and feelings. Each of these categories is like taking a snap-shot of a different kaleidoscope pattern. Yet all of these patterns have places that overlap. *Inequality* could be described as a state where one person's needs are consistently more important than the other's. Inequality is also when one person shoulders more of the burden of responsibility than the other. Resentment is inevitable in either case.

One of my clients works long hours for moderate pay, then comes home to fix dinner, bathe the children, oversee homework and bedtimes, and fix tomorrow's lunches. Her partner works part-time at a low paying job, spends a good deal of his salary on beer, and complains if dinner isn't served on time. She feels trapped because she needs what little money he contributes to help pay for household expenses, and yet she longs to break out of a relationship that traps both of them in an unhealthy, codependent dance. The total responsibilities of the partnership, including parenting, are unequally divided. The resentment generated creates a huge barrier in their relationship.

An incredible example of *inappropriate involvement* was reported in the newspapers some time ago. A professional athlete was very unhappy with the amount of playing time he was being given. Finally, his wife went to management on his behalf. I doubt that her husband knew what she was doing. As soon as possible, the manager transferred this pro to the other side of the country to play for another team!

One young couple came to me in desperate trouble. She was complaining about her husband to co-workers, friends, and her grandmother, asking one and all for advice. He was moaning to his parents and siblings. I suggested that they cease all talk about their relationship other than, respectfully, with each other, a counselor, and perhaps their pastor. They chose, instead, to dissipate their energy on complaining sessions with multiple others—energy that could have gone toward the building of a successful relationship. There was nothing seriously wrong with the relationship that focused attention couldn't have corrected; yet in a few short months divorce proceedings were begun. They had invited many others to be inappropriately involved.

ENMESHMENT RATHER THAN RELATIONSHIP

Many wedding ceremonies include the words, "the two shall be one…" Indeed, two persons in a highly functioning, healthy marriage seem to work together with nearly seamless unity. Isn't that what a good marriage should be? Each dependent on the other, both keeping up their ends of the relationship?

Yes and no. This simple analogy comes to mind. A shoelace is a single entity, one string, united in one purpose—to hold a shoe snuggly against the foot. After being inserted in the bottom eyes of the shoe, it is divided in half. As both halves zig-zag through the eyes and meet at the top, then cooperate in the tying of a knot and bow, they successfully fulfill their purpose of being together. Although the lace is one, the two halves function interdependently. (Remember interdependence from Chapter 1?)

If the laces become double knotted together, stuck in a tangled mess, they have lost their ability to cooperate. Now they are locked in an embrace that, rather than being functional, is more like being imprisoned. When this happens in a relationship, the discomfort of the tangled knots becomes the focus of their energy rather than the teamwork that could move them toward mutually beneficial goals.

In a healthy relationship, each half of the shoestring is being fully responsible for its job, and working in easy cooperation with the other half, which is also fully responsible for its job. There is mutual sharing, mutual responsibility, a give and take in the investment of time and attention. Sometimes the circumstances of life may dictate that one person's needs are temporarily primary; but perhaps, at some later time, the other person's needs may require more attention. Each is willing *for a period of time* to shoulder more of the load for the other . . . but not indefinitely. Not if both persons are well and capable.

A true friendship is mutually supportive and enjoyable. When one friend is consistently the one supporting and the other is habitually needy, there is an imbalance of benefits.

There is a normal, expected imbalance of responsibility between a parent and child. There is no doubt that a child needs more support than the parent. Yet, this relationship is also subject to imbalance in either direction. On the one hand, the parent may be so needy that the child becomes the responsible party. On the other extreme, the parent is so committed to meeting every possible desire of the child that the parent's needs are ignored. Sometimes both parents are so involved in the life of their child or children that the needs of the marriage are ignored... or presumed less important.

Correcting the above examples of enmeshment often creates a temporary upheaval in the relationship. The one who was getting the lion's share of attention may resent the cutback. The one who wants to reorder his or her priorities, often feels guilty for, in essence, saying, "My needs are important, also." The emotions that are being triggered are characteristics of moving away from an entanglement and toward a healthier balance in the relationship. Both parties are poised on the edge of difficult conflict or fantastic growth. Sometimes the initial conflict (resistance to change) is the doorway through which fantastic growth is found. The ultimate outcome depends on one's readiness to be responsible for one's self.

Results: resentment!

Many, probably even most, romantic relationships begin as a tangled enmeshment surrounded by a soft cloud of romantic love and sexual energy. The long-term purpose of the relationship usually becomes apparent at some later time when the unconscious agendas of each partner begin to result in unfulfilled expectations—and resentment.

As an enabler, my resentment comes from believing that I am a victim . . . that I am powerless. I have surrendered my power to someone else, allowing that person to dictate the quality of my life. I have chosen the role of helplessness. In childhood I may, indeed, have been helpless. For some of us, reclaiming the power to make our own choices in life requires courageous steps, often requiring the support of a counselor, trusted mentor, or support group.

Authentic personal power doesn't grandstand or berate another or explode in ways that damage or destroy. My first attempts to claim authentic power, however, were quite awkward. Those hesitant steps into self-responsibility didn't look particularly graceful or dignified; but they were a beginning—a beginning as precious and exciting as watching a baby learning to walk.

When I stopped rescuing Steve from the consequences of his choices, he didn't immediately thank me for treating him like a capable adult. His first response was disbelief. His mother had become unpredictable. His next emotion was anger. Finally he became resigned to being responsible for himself. Eventually, I was fortunate that he became grateful. I'll share more about that at the end of this book.

My beginning steps were fearful and hesitant, hoping I was still a good mother. The emotions of fear and insecurity soon morphed into a sense of freedom from the codependent chains that kept me tied to Steven in ways that were unhealthy for both of us. I soon realized that I no longer needed his approval to know I was a good mother...or a loving person. The liberation and jump in my self-esteem felt a little heady!

If I'm the one who is irresponsible, expecting someone else to pick up the mess left by me, I feel resentment. That person is no longer passively agreeing with my demands or putting up with the results of my irresponsibility. For some reason, it seems to be universally easier to see ourselves as the victim rather than the abuser. In the early days of my marriage to Jim, I felt resentment when he walked away rather than "take" my verbal abuse! I did not want to see his behavior as a natural consequence of my irresponsible expression of anger!

It takes great courage to examine the source of resentment and evaluate the cause as my choice of being the *victim*, or my unwillingness to give up *victimizing*.

One of the most frequent by-products of resentment is *depression*. Depression often comes when resentment is "stuffed" or abusively expressed to another. I was depressed not only from stuffing my resentment toward Jim, but from my disappointment in myself for the way I was acting.

Resentment also creates *distance* in the relationship. Every time I submit to being treated disrespectfully without being truthful about how I feel, a block is added to the barrier. Every time I treat my partner disrespectfully, another block is added. Every time the truth is not spoken the wall becomes thicker.

When the emotional distance in a relationship seems impenetrable, some become so lonely that the relationship is abandoned in search of emotional connection with another. At the time, it may seem easier to leave than doing the work of removing the blocks and closing the emotional distance in *this* relationship. There are circumstances where the relationship is so toxic that it is irredeemable and *must* be left. If the one leaving doesn't do the work of identifying his or her contribution to the toxicity, however, a similarly unhealthy relationship is likely to be created with someone new.

Resentment also gives birth to *disillusionment*. So many of the couples I see are children of unhappy or divorced parents. Each couple enters marriage with an ideal of what they hope to achieve. But lacking successful role models, they aren't sure how to create the loving, respectful partnership they crave. When issues arise between the partners, these couples often have the resigned belief that it was inevitable. One of the most frequent feedback remarks I get after teaching a workshop is gratitude that I am so transparent about the problems I've experienced in relationships, what I learned, and put into practice that gave me the relationships I wanted. After practicing the skills I teach, many couples sigh with relief because now they know they can make their marriages work "'till death do us part."

Other clients who are equally deserving of healthy, loving relationships, find that the only way to be healthy, is to leave the marriage, friendship or family. Sometimes this means leaving unrealistic expectations. Other times it means establishing limits of contact. In some cases, the only sane course is physical separation from a relationship. Dr. Henry Cloud has done a good job of addressing these options in his book, *Necessary Endings: The Employees, Businesses, and Relationships That All of Us Have to Give Up in Order to Move Forward.*

A CHECK LIST

Here's another list of symptoms to help you identify the BARRIERs of codependency from Gay and Kathlyn Hendricks in their book, *Conscious Loving: The Journey to Co-Commitment.*

"Ask yourself whether you have some of the following issues in your relationships:

- ❑ In spite of your "best efforts," people around you do not change their bad habits.
- ❑ You have difficulty allowing others to feel their feelings. If someone feels bad, you rush in to make it better. You frequently worry about other people's feelings.
- ❑ You do not let yourself feel the full range of your feelings. You are out of touch with one or more core emotions such as anger, fear, or sadness. Anger is a particular problem for you. You find it hard to admit that you're angry. And you have trouble expressing it (appropriately) to other people.

❑ You criticize or get criticized frequently. You have a strong, nagging internal critic that keeps you feeling bad even in moments when you could be feeling good.

❑ You try to control other people, to get them to feel and be a certain way, and you spend a lot of energy being controlled or avoiding being controlled by others.

❑ Your arguments tend to recycle. Conflicts are temporarily ended by one person apologizing and promising to do better.

❑ In arguments, much energy is spent in trying to find out whose fault it is. Both people struggle to prove that they are right, or to prove the other wrong.

❑ In arguments, you find yourself pleading as a victim or agreeing that you were at fault.

❑ You frequently agree to do things you do not want to do, feel bad about it, but say nothing.

❑ People seem not to keep their agreements with you."

SUMMARY

Where does codependency erect a barrier? Codependency erects a BARRIER between me and the other person, whether partner, child, friend or co-worker, making it impossible to experience a healthy balance of responsibility, respect, and, when appropriate, love. It's that simple.

STIR THE POTION: Deconstructing the BARRIER

With which characteristics, descriptions or stories in this chapter do you relate to most strongly? What are you becoming aware of in yourself? A tendency to assume too much responsibility, a tendency to assume too little responsibility, or both? Are you beginning to identify a place where you'd like to change your pattern of behavior? What might be your first step? What are you feeling? Do you need more support? Where might you look for healthy support as you deconstruct the barriers created by codependency?

Chapter 6: FEAR VS LOVE

I believe that all interactions in relationships come from a source that is either fear based or love based. In my personal experiences, and the experiences explored with my clients, codependent behaviors originate from fear masquerading as love.

In the preview to this book, I told about my saga with the carpenter. I was timid about holding him to his contract with me because I was afraid of being thought of as "bitchy," the opposite being a "good" woman. It was only when I realized that supporting his lies was not really "nice," that I made a boundary to encourage him to keep his word to me and finish my job. The boundary I set was definitely loving toward myself as it facilitated the meeting of my reasonable needs. It was also loving to refuse to support behaviors in him that were not in his best interests as a person or as a businessman.

In Chapter 2 where I shared about Steven's California Missions Project fiasco, I pitched in and rescued him from a poor grade because I was afraid of my child being labeled a poor student. I was also afraid that if I allowed him to suffer painful consequences that I could prevent, I would be a "bad" mother. My fears prompted me to choose a course of action that was not in Steven's long term best interests. I prevented him from learning some valuable life lessons, such as planning ahead, and breaking a big job into little pieces completed over time in order to make a deadline. In that example, choices made from fear hurt both of us.

Many poor parenting decisions are made when a parent wants a child to "behave" in order to validate the parent's competence as a "good" parent. When Steve's misbehaviors became more public, I was frantic to hide them or get past them quickly so that, perhaps, no one would hear about them. Bailing him out of jail, finding a new high school when he was expelled, (three times) going to a court appointed counselor when he was arrested for selling stolen property, paying some guys off who were injured in an accident caused by Steve, were all scenes from my worst nightmares. I felt exposed. I felt stripped naked in public. I assumed the full burden of failure…feelings that many parents experience when their kid is in trouble.

Although there is no doubt that I loved Steve through all of this, most of my choices were driven by fear, not love: absolute terror that his life was being ruined and I couldn't stop it; fear that he would kill himself with his careless disregard for safety; awareness of the pain he was in that I, and multiple counselors, were powerless to alleviate; fear that I really was a bad mother; fear of the judgments being levied against me by friends and family; fear that the ultimate blame for his bad choices truly rested with me, alone; fear that I'd never discover the key to unlocking his addictions to set him free.

I was so fear driven, and the episodes happened so frequently that I couldn't seem to breathe. Just before his eighteenth birthday, I forcibly committed him to a rehab facility. He was livid. Enraged. I was hopeful that this program might get him turned around, and, truthfully, glad to have his destructive presence out of the house for a few months.

He passively followed instructions and worked the program. While there, he turned eighteen. I was asked if I'd allow him to return home after completing the program. I intuitively knew that the moment he was released, he would dive head-long into his addiction. I said he couldn't come home to live. He could come during daylight hours and eat whatever we had in the house, but he couldn't come, even in the daytime, to "crash" after a drug binge (sleep it off).

He picked up odd jobs, crashed at a friend's house, often slept in his car, and looked like death warmed over. Every time I saw him, and then hugged him goodbye, I'd think, "I may never see him alive again." It was excruciating. My heart was breaking. But I was learning what all recovering codependents in relationship with dedicated addicts eventually learn, that I cannot "save" another. He must save himself. I can love him, care about him, and want the best for him, but I do not need to prove my love by allowing the chaos of *his* life choices to dominate *my* life.

There's no doubt that I made many mistakes in parenting Steven. But I also did a lot of things very well. It is typical of codependents to assume *all* the responsibility, *all* the blame, *all* the shame. It was years before I could see that Steve *chose* to lie, steal, and use drugs. I did not model that lifestyle for him. Nor did I ever, in any way, encourage those choices. A large part of my disconnection from codependent behaviors was letting go of responsibilities that were not rightfully mine, but were Steve's alone. As I did so, I began to define myself in terms *other* than my child's behavior.

In Steve's mid-twenties, I told him, "I love you. I'll always love you no matter what you do or decide. When you are ready to get help, if you want me to, I'll help you find the best help possible. But until then, your choices and the consequences that come with them, are yours alone. I will be all right no matter what you decide." Steven told me later how liberating those words were for him. From then on he was responsible only for himself. My ultimate well-being would not rise and fall with his choices.

Being in a relationship with him continued to be a challenge. The lessons continued right up until his death and beyond. His choices certainly brought the consequence to me of enormous grief. But my self-worth and value were no longer tied to his behavior. We were both set free from the bonds of enmeshment.

Note: Recent research sheds light on predisposing conditions that prime some persons for addictive behaviors. It seems that certain predispositions may make some persons more vulnerable to addictions than others. You may want to learn more about the latest addiction science by Nora D. Volkow, M.D., the director of the National Institute of Drug Abuse at http://www.drugabuse.gov/ Her work is easy to understand and seems impossible to refute. A cure for addiction may be on the horizon.

SYMPATHY VS. EMPATHY

There is a difference between sympathy and empathy. Sympathy is feeling bad because she feels bad, internalizing her feelings as though they are my own and drowning in them *with* her. Sympathy often leads to efforts to "fix" the situation so that the pain goes away for both persons. Empathy is caring that she is in pain, even stepping into the other's shoes and imagining how I would feel in the same situation. But empathy does not assume responsibility for those feelings.

Sympathy is often characterized by pity or "feeling sorry for" the other. Pity perceives the other as a victim, weak, and helpless. Decisions made because you pity someone, or feel sorry for him or her, are unfailingly codependent, and thereby, unhealthy for both the giver and receiver. Choices to "help" another when motivated from pity, invariably weaken the recipient. Pity never builds up, but tears down the one on the receiving end of your "caring."

Empathy recognizes that, although the pain is uncomfortable, it may be necessary for her to experience, (such as grief after a loss) or it may be needed to stimulate personal growth, (such as the embarrassment of being fired for chronic lateness, or the humiliation of being betrayed by someone that she already knew was untrustworthy). Empathy takes appropriate action when others need temporary or long term care. Empathy strengthens the recipient of care with dignity. Empathy sees and cares about the pain, but makes sure that helpful actions do not rob the individual of the strengthening process gained by doing all he is capable of for himself.

A PERSONAL ASIDE

I particularly like and support charities that not only deliver appropriate help, but pair the help with education and the expectation that individuals and communities use that help to become self-sustaining, thereby building dignity and responsibility into the assistance.

- World Vision, an organization with a flawless record of responsible money management, feeds and educates children, provides clean water wells in rural villages, and offers adult education for both men and women to help them be self-supporting, (www.worldvision.org)
- Heifer, International (www.heifer.org) gives animals to families trained to care for them with the understanding that the animal's first offspring will be given to another village family along with training for it's care. These animals provide milk, cheese, eggs and offspring that can significantly increase a family's health as well as yearly income.
- One Acre Fund (www.oneacrefund.org) distributes seed and fertilizer to the world's poor who are primarily farmers along with training on agricultural techniques and marketing to maximize profits from produce sales.
- Central Asia Institute (www.ikat.org) in partnership with tribal leaders, empowers women in remote areas of Afghanistan, Pakistan and Tajikistan by building and supporting local schools. They've found that when a woman is educated, the whole village is elevated because women share their knowledge. Health issues and the influence of the Taliban are both reduced when women are educated.

There are certainly more charities worthy of support. Perhaps because my father was a vegetable farmer I am drawn to those organizations that help eliminate hunger and elevate living conditions through farming. In addition, I am so grateful for the educational opportunities that have improved my life.

EVERYDAY EXAMPLES

One morning my late husband Jim woke up on the wrong side of the bed. He was grumpy to begin with, and then everything went wrong. He growled when the hot water ran out during his shower. He loudly complained when he nicked himself shaving. As I walked by the bathroom door, I said, "I'm sorry you're having such a tough morning," and kept going.

In the past, I would have tried to find something I could do to make it better. I might have asked, "Would your favorite breakfast turn things around for you today?" I might have told him a funny story to get his mind off of his troubles. *I* would have assumed responsibility for changing *his* mood. Instead, I went on about my morning chores and trusted that he was adult enough to deal with his own emotions.

Jim and I talked about it later. He noticed how I'd handled his upset because it was so different than my usual "helpful" routine. He said how liberating it was for him. In the past, when I would try to "fix" something for him, he felt responsible, not only for his *own* upset, but for trying to snap out of it so that *I* would feel better.

He woke up grumpy. I try to fix him. He then, tries to get happy, not only to relieve his own feelings, but to relieve mine. Do you see why codependency creates enmeshment? Not relationship! Do you see why the analogy of "Velcro" is so apt for when two persons get caught up in each other's dramas?

A teenage daughter was expressing hormonal fluxuations by griping about everything to everyone else in the household. Her dad demonstrated a healthy response by telling her, "You may not be able to help how you feel, but you *can* control how you act. Go to your room until you find the self-control to be civil to your family." Yay, Dad!

TWO FEARS

What is at the core of my decision to rescue someone in distress that was brought on by their own choices? Two fears that masquerade as love: (1) Fear that he can't handle the feelings, the situation or the consequences of his choices without my help, (So demeaning a belief!) and, (2) fear that I'm not a good (loving, kind, caring) person unless I help her recover her good nature, (meaning that somehow it's my fault if she isn't happy all the time). Those two fears are what drive many codependent choices.

LOVE

Loving myself is: acknowledging that my needs and feelings are as important as anyone else's; assuming responsibility for my choices and their consequences; maintaining a healthy awareness of what responsibilities are mine vs. those that belong to another; questioning the source of my decisions to ensure that they are coming from love, not fear or pity; appropriately protecting myself from the blame, shame, and abuse of others; accepting that my value is intrinsic to who I am and does not have to be earned by being subservient to another; cooperating in relationships that are interdependent, where individual assets are pooled for the betterment of all, and with responsibilities equally distributed; and, no doubt, more…

Loving another is: allowing him or her the dignity and freedom of his or her (age appropriate) choices without trying to "fix" them; recognizing that I am, indeed, powerless to dictate the quality of life or life decisions for another; care-giving when it is needed, but only to the degree that it strengthens the other, rather than robbing the recipient of dignity or strength; holding the other accountable to their agreements or promises; refusing to allow, facilitate or in any way encourage deception, dishonesty or abuse by another; stopping the impulse to rescue another from the natural consequences of his or her choices; allowing others the dignity of their life-paths, the lessons designed for their growth; and, no doubt, more…

SUMMARY

Relationship decisions borne from a source of fear are rarely, if ever, healthy for either party. Learning to recognize the source of our choices is a gigantic step toward disconnecting from the enmeshment of codependency. Giving others the dignity of experiencing the consequences of their choices is genuinely loving and life-affirming. We are designed to learn from our experiences. It is only possible to genuinely love another person *to the degree I love myself.* Anything less might appear on the surface to be love, but may be an unconscious bid for approval, value, meaning or love. Choices made from authentic love are *always* healthier and more empowering to both parties.

STIR THE POT: Fear vs. Love

As you've read this chapter, what awareness have you had about the motivation for one or two of your relationship decisions? Do you recognize any decision in the past or present that was driven by fear? What were or are you afraid of? What can you identify that resulted from that choice? For yourself? For the other?

Chapter 7: BOUNDARIES

I'm proposing a distinction between rules and boundaries. There is some overlap in their definitions, but for the purposes of this volume, I'd like to emphasize the differences as they apply to codependency.

Rules are cultural. Rules are designed to control or bring order to a family, a culture or a community. They vary from country to country, state to state, family to family. Learning to eat with a fork rather than with your fingers is a Western cultural expectation. In the Western world, if you eat with your fingers, you'll probably be ostracized... or at least thought of as uncouth. Western custom is to shake hands when meeting or leaving a colleague. Hugs or pats might be more appropriate for a friend or family member. We learn to brush our teeth morning and night to prevent cavities. It's a law that children must be fed, housed, and go to school. There's also a strong cultural expectation that children be loved and nurtured emotionally. Family rules teach us how to gain acceptance and be loved in a particular family. Civic rules govern behavior by punishing infractions with fines or prison sentences.

The examples given above are either legal or cultural or both. Rules teach us to behave in ways which open doors of acceptance in the particular family or community in which we live. Rules may be expressly defined or simply be "the way it's always been done" or "the way it's done in our family." Rules may be reasonable or unreasonable, fair or unfair, generally healthy, or not, either in a family or in a culture.

Boundaries, as defined in this book, are different from rules. Boundaries are designed to protect one from the irresponsible or abusive behavior of another. Boundaries do not control the other's behavior but limit the contact or effect of the other's behavior on oneself with the goal of one's physical and/or emotional well-being. Boundaries are created to differentiate between one's responsibilities and another's. The intention is that boundaries are morally and emotionally healthy for every party involved, whether others like them or not. Boundaries honor oneself *and* the other. Boundaries treat oneself and the other with dignity and respect. Boundaries give each person the freedom of his or her choices *and* their consequences. At times, boundaries may conflict with rules.

BOUNDARIES VS. RULES

A historical example of when boundaries conflicted with rules happened during World War II. The rule (law) was that certain members of society must be sent to "camps" for labor and ultimate extermination. Many persons and communities held to the ethical, humanitarian boundary of respect for life to the point that persons in danger of imprisonment were hidden or smuggled out of dangerous areas at great risk to the rule-breaker.

Many who rejected the right of Germany to dominate Europe worked underground to further the allied cause. One rule-breaking act was to smuggle downed pilots, one of whom was my uncle, from behind enemy lines to safety. The rule-breakers' belief in the ultimate right of his or her country to be self-governing, trumped the current law.

It's difficult for a friend of mine to straddle the line between her Anglo-American father's expectations (rules) and her Japanese mother's expectations (rules.) Her father expects her to be independent, capable in the family business, and tough as nails. Her mother's family rules passed down through generations of subservient Japanese women, dictate that she "serve" her mother and the extended family. After being torn between conflicting rules for many years, my friend is learning to set self-honoring, loving boundaries with both her mother and father. While never neglecting her love and respect for either of them, the more she honors her needs with reasonable boundaries, the less resentment she feels. Neither her mother nor father like that my friend is "breaking" the respective family rules, but as they adjust to the new boundaries, there is less and less conflict. The boundaries she is enforcing with her parents are healthy for all of them, even though initially uncomfortable.

RESENTMENT: A RULE OF THUMB

You may remember from *Chapter 5: THE INVISIBLE BARRIER*, that the result of codependency is resentment. Resentment kills relationships. Jim and I realized that whenever we did something for each other in spite of resenting it, we noticed distance between us...the barrier. We made an agreement to never do anything the other asked, if in doing that favor, the giver felt resentment. By eliminating resentment from our interactions, we also eliminated codependent behaviors.

Neither of us took this to the extreme. The "resentment rule of thumb" does not apply to every minor irritation. If Jim asked for a favor and I felt momentary annoyance that immediately disappeared when I recalled how he'd sweetly walked my dog for me yesterday, I would do the favor without resentment.

This "resentment rule of thumb" does not mean that I'm unwilling to learn new habits that will benefit the other person and better the relationship. For instance, giving compliments or words of affirmation or appreciation did not come naturally to me. But when I learned that Jim's primary love language was *words of affirmation,* I forced myself to get good at giving him those positive words. Although it was difficult to develop that habit, I did so because I wanted Jim to know how much I loved him and *words of affirmation* was the language that was the most effective way of delivering my love to him.

I may initially resent the work of changing a habit, but changing a behavior in me that would benefit my partner and the relationship, is excluded from this "rule of thumb." The payoff of overcoming this cause of resentment is a better relationship for *me*, as well as for him!

When Jim and I agreed on a guideline for his son's behavior, but he didn't follow through with enforcing it, (and this happened repeatedly) persistent resentment took root in me. As my resentment grew, my respect for him dwindled. This was a deep and long-lasting resentment that had to be addressed. Resolving this source of deep resentment was one of the key pieces that enabled us to successfully save our marriage.

Similarly, I spoke to a friend this week whose husband's love language is touch. She is not naturally a touching or an easily sexual person, but she makes sure to warmly touch, hug, stroke, massage and respond to him sexually because she knows that is the best way to convey to this man that he is loved. (Determine your love language and the love language of your loved ones by each taking the free online quiz at www.5lovelanguages.com/profile/)

On a lighter note, when Jim invited me to attend a Lakers Basketball Game in Los Angeles where he was scheduled to sing the National Anthem, I asked him, "On a scale of one to ten, how important is it that I go with you?" When he answered, "One," I declined. I would have gone if his answer had been seven or above, I really didn't want to go. He invited others who were far more appreciative of the opportunity than I was. (I'd heard him sing the National Anthem at Angels Baseball games multiple times.)

When my aging parents needed more attention, part of me resented the time and energy it took. I was already caring for a terminally ill son, attending school to earn my master's degree, managing our home and maintaining a healthy marriage. But I realized that I could not neglect my parents without violating my own code of honor or integrity. I was fortunate to have three sisters with whom to share those responsibilities and ultimately grateful to do my part to ensure my parents' had loving care.

To never agree to or tolerate a behavior when it created deep-seated resentment became a healthy agreement that governed my relationship with Jim and, coincidently, eliminated codependency. Eventually that guideline or "rule of thumb" generalized to other relationships and situations helping me to make choices that were self-honoring in all areas of my life. Persistent, deep-seated resentment poisons both you and the relationship in which it is experienced.

SETTING BOUNDARIES=BREAKING THE RULES

It would be easy to set reasonable boundaries to protect ourselves from those who would take advantage, hurt or abuse us if, in setting those boundaries, we did not have to go up against some inner or outer "rule." The rules were embedded in our psyches from family or cultural patterns or beliefs we've internalized, or a definition of love that we've misunderstood. The work of setting a healthy boundary is the work of breaking a rule or challenging a belief that no longer serves one's wellbeing. The following example will illustrate.

IN RELATIONSHIP WITH AN ACTIVE ADDICT

Most codependency information came out of the growing understanding of the relationship dynamics surrounding addictions, either drug or alcohol. The example that follows is classic as experienced in relationship with an addict. Examples of codependency that are common to us all are explored in Chapter 8.

When Angie married Dan, she had no idea he was addicted to cocaine. Dan's cocaine use was not a daily, or even a weekly occurrence. Every few months, Dan would disappear for a few days, immersed in a cocaine binge. Angie soon became familiar with the routine: the anguish of not knowing if he was alive or dead; the fear of how much money would disappear this time; the loneliness of waiting; the shame of finding herself married to a drug addict, a role she never, in her wildest imagination, thought would be true of her; the rage when he returned home looking like a derelict; the fruitless attempts to protect their limited assets; the exhausting process of "cleaning up the mess" after each binge; the fear of others finding out that led to lies to their families, employers and friends; the dashed hopes after multiple attempts at recovery; the desolation of her failure to be enough to motivate Dan to kick his habit; her self-judgment and terror that others were judging her as stupid for staying with him.

When "clean," Dan was extremely intelligent, thoughtful, repentant, a good provider, a man with a good heart—someone with whom she would choose, again, to spend the rest of her life. Angie thought that if he'd been a consistently practicing addict, or a jerk, or abusive, she would have left him without question, although many who find themselves in relationship with chronic addicts are not able to leave.

Over a period of years, Angie learned of her role in the addiction dynamic from family counseling during rehab attempts, attendance at Codependents Anonymous support groups and, eventually from my coaching. She gradually began to face the fears, family rules and beliefs that kept her imprisoned by Dan's choices. She became less willing to be the "good wife" and clean up the post-binge messes, worked at becoming more financially independent, and was increasingly more supportive of her right to plan a life for herself that included the stability she craved. She began to release the shame she felt about being married to an addict, recognizing that it was Dan who had lied, deceived, stolen their assets and jeopardized their future together. These things were his responsibilities, not hers. She accepted her part in the codependent dance when she lied to her family and others, and worked harder to control Dan's addiction than she worked at taking care of herself. As much as she loved Dan, she courageously examined whether she wanted to gamble on him with her life and the lives of the children she wanted in her future.

A few months after their tenth anniversary, and eight months after his last episode, Dan "went out" for four days. This time Angie ate and slept better than before, almost continuously releasing Dan and herself into God's loving care. When Dan returned, she lovingly told him she was glad he was home safe. She calmly added, however, that she would stay in a motel for the next three nights because she would not put herself through the torture of watching while his body tried to recover from the devastation of the binge. She spent those three nights alone, got a massage, went to see some movies, prayed a lot, and discovered that she could survive without Dan.

A few days later, they met in my office. With kindness, compassion, and extraordinary clarity she delivered this message to Dan, "I love you. I will always love you. I feel compassion for your struggle with cocaine, but I deserve to have the life I want. I want a home of my own and children with a man I can depend on to be there for us. You have until the end of this year (about ten months) to demonstrate that you are doing everything within your power to permanently kick this addiction and help me build the life I want. That means doing the recovery work you've been unwilling to do in the past and saving enough money so that we can buy a house and plan for a child. If, at the end of this year, I can't see enough progress, then I will leave you. I am still young enough to find someone who will help me build a stable life and have a family."

The words were delivered with tenderness, but with clear boundaries. Setting this boundary meant that Angie broke the rule of being the patient, supportive, always believing wife. She was no longer willing to see herself as the helpless victim of Dan's choices. Setting this boundary with Dan also meant that she was ready to face her family's disapproval of divorce. She broke the code of silence and informed her family of the current situation…and then calmly handled their rage at Dan and disapproval of Angie for staying with him. Angie set this boundary with the power of her conviction that she deserved what she wanted. The words rang with the sound of freedom—freedom from bitterness and victimhood.

Dan had not come to the meeting empty-handed. He had already begun taking the steps he'd previously resisted. He joined a highly successful, local recovery program, *Celebrate Recovery*, a Christian Twelve Step Program that is now available nationwide. Rather than hanging out on the fringes of the meetings as he had before, he began making friends, exchanging phone numbers, and sharing more honestly in the group. He is determined to be a man of integrity in all areas of his life. He began treating himself with more kindness, rather than the self-loathing he nurtured in the past.

Their struggles were not magically over. Dan went through a period of abusing alcohol rather than cocaine. His health began to fail due to the years of chemical abuse. They both had to set boundaries with their extended families to stop the expression to them of criticism, judgment and self-righteous advice giving. Gradually they found their way through the mire.

As of this writing, Dan is clean from both drugs and alcohol. Together they have faced health, job and financial challenges. They have two beautiful children. Dan is enjoying being the kind of involved, emotionally present father that he wished he had experienced as a child. Both Dan and Angie continue to manage their extended family relationships within boundaries that give them the safety they need. Dan continues in therapy, learning more and more about the antecedents and management of his addictive tendencies. Recently he told me that he regrets all the pain his choices caused those he loves, especially Angie, but doesn't regret the lessons learned that brought him to this very rich time in his life. Angie and their children are thriving in their hard-won stability and the trustworthiness, love and leadership qualities that Dan now brings to the family.

NANCY'S QUESTIONS THAT CLARIFY SOURCES OF RESENTMENT
When I feel resentful:
Have I assumed a responsibility that isn't rightfully mine? Whose problem is it?
Have I assumed more responsibility than is my fair share?
Am I trying to "save" a loved one from experiencing the consequences of his or her choices?
Have I agreed to contribute more of myself (energy, time, or emotions) than I can gladly give?
Am I helping or giving to someone else to the detriment or neglect of my own needs?
Do I want the other person to change his or her behavior so I won't have to change mine?
(In my experience this last question is frequently the biggy!)

When someone is angry with me:
Do I expect this person to tolerate my irresponsibility?
Have I expected this person to fulfill my responsibility *for* me?
Am I expecting that this person suffer consequences that are rightfully mine?
Do I expect this person to "fix" a situation for me or provide a solution?
(The first four questions might be answered "yes" when I am trying to get away with irresponsibility.)

Or,

Is this person angry because I have chosen not to "rescue" him or her as I have in the past?

Is this person angry because I will not agree to be victim to his or her neglect or abuse?

Is this person angry because I refuse to support, encourage, or participate in his or her self-abusive or irresponsible behavior?

Is this person angry because I cannot make him or her feel better or fix this person's problem?

(These questions might be answered "yes" when I am refusing to play a codependent role in relationship to him or her. In this case, the anger is to be expected and not anything I need apologize for or try to "fix.")

This prayer repeated in most 12-step meetings is so appropriate for the process of recovery from codependency: "God, grant me the Serenity to accept the things I cannot change; Courage to change the things I can; and Wisdom to know the difference. Living one day at a time, enjoying one moment at a time; Accepting hardship as a pathway to peace; Taking, as Jesus did, this sinful world as it is; Not as I would have it; Trusting that You will make all things right if I surrender to Your will; So that I may be reasonably happy in this life And supremely happy with You forever in the next. Amen." By Reinhold Niebuhr.

SUMMARY

For the purposes of this book, rules and boundaries have different purposes. The purpose of rules is to train or control a family or community. The purpose of a boundary is to protect oneself from the hurtful behavior of another. Setting a personal boundary is often hard because internally adopted or externally expected rules must be confronted. The process of examining and then challenging currently held rules often requires the neutral support of a group like Codependents Anonymous, a counselor or coach. It's unrealistic to expect others to like or cooperate with a new boundary, even though it may be introducing healthier dynamics to the relationship. Boundaries that release one from codependency bring increased self-worth and liberation from resentment and victimhood.

STIR THE POT: Setting a Boundary

Choose one thing for which you feel persistent resentment toward someone. What are you trying to make him or her do? Which of your needs or wants are you holding him or her responsible for meeting? What methods are you using to try to change him or her? Is your current strategy producing the result you want? Are you willing to try something different? The next chapter offers some options!

Chapter 8: OPTIONS

I love this quote by Albert Einstein, "We cannot solve the problems we have at the same level of thinking we were at when we created them." Another way of conveying the same truth is, "If we continue to do what we've always done, we'll continue to get what we've always gotten." A third popular quote expressing this life lesson is, "Insanity is doing the same thing over and over again while expecting a different result."

As you've read the previous pages you may have identified your codependent behaviors in more than one relationship. I recommend that you begin your codependent recovery by choosing just one relationship to address. Perhaps it will be the relationship where you have the least to risk—the relationship that is least essential to you. Or you may go for the one where the resentment is such a hard knot in your chest that you can barely breathe. So where do you begin?

OPTION ONE: A SKILLED DISCUSSION
Ask for a *Skilled Discussion* with this person. Use all the guidelines taught in **Communication Elixirs,** and reviewed in **Savory Safeguards**. Prepare for this discussion as though you are studying for a big exam. Use the "Planning What to Say" form included in the free download work sheets on my website. (See **YOU ARE INVITED...**)

Know your goal. Your goal is to eliminate the situation or behavior that feeds your resentment. You may have an idea of the change you want to have happen or a different, but an equally effective solution may emerge from this discussion. Ideally, the other person may agree to change the behavior. That promise of change needs to be supported by the reinforcing and reward steps described in **Savory Safeguards** and there must be logical consequences if this person doesn't follow through with genuine, measurable steps toward permanent change.

Start with something good about this person or the value to you of this relationship. Remember to stick with "I…" messages, not accusatory "You…." statements. An example is, "When (this) happens, I feel resentful."

The purpose of using the *Skilled Dialogue* format is to be heard by the Listener with some degree of understanding, and so be certain to eliminate words that might trigger defensiveness or escalate this discussion into an argument. When the other person speaks, use the *Listen to Understand* skill by repeating back in your own words what has been said. You may not do this with every sentence, but summarize what he or she has said to reassure him or her that you're listening.

Then go back to speaking your truth. After sharing your thoughts and feelings, name your concern. That might be, "The resentment I feel is damaging to our relationship. Resentment is making it hard for me to remember how much I love you (or care for you, or care for this relationship.)"

Ask for what you want. Ask clearly and specifically. General requests are subject to misinterpretation. General requests are things such as, "I want more help around the house," or, "I want to be treated with respect." Specific requests are, "I've made a list of household chores. Would you be willing to assume responsibility for three of these?" Or, "When we're in a social gathering, are you willing to stop making critical comments about me?"

If you get a "yes" to your request, see if this person is willing to brainstorm reminders that don't feel like nagging to him or her, and find out how you can reinforce the change in behavior in a way that he or she likes. Refer to the *Problem Solving Worksheet* described in detail in **Savory**

Safeguards and included in the free download pages offered at www. nancylandrum.com That worksheet maps out problem solving strategies that greatly increase your chances that this solution will be successful.

EXAMPLES

When my late husband Jim and I were just beginning to learn the skills that helped us save our marriage, I chose one of the few issues that was relatively small in order to practice doing a *Skilled Dialogue.* The issue was which one of us gets to park in the garage and which one must park on the street. Jim had no idea that this was even an issue for me. His car was nicer and newer so he'd been parking in the garage. I worked at a job that necessitated frequently hauling a lot of equipment around, and I was the grocery shopper. I would carry the equipment or groceries in and out of the house from the street, loading and unloading depending on where I was going or coming from, or how many kids I was hauling around.

I started with, "You are so thoughtful about so many things. I appreciate the quality of thoughtfulness in you." I went on to say, "When I have to carry equipment or groceries in and out of the house from the street, I feel resentful that I'm not the one who parks in the garage. I carry things four times farther than I would have to if I parked in the garage. I don't like feeling resentment toward you. Would you be willing to change parking spaces with me?"

Jim was astonished. He repeated back what I'd said. When it was his turn to speak, he said, "I'm so sorry. I've been oblivious about how much extra work you have to do by parking in the street. We'll switch immediately!"

My mother was quite forceful about insisting or expecting that all family members converge on her house for holidays. One year Jim and I especially wanted to host our children, spouses and first grandchild at our home for Thanksgiving. I was nervous about telling my mother we wouldn't be joining THE FAMILY at her home. I carefully planned what to say and braced myself for her disappointment and the resulting guilt trip.

I called. When she answered, I said, "Mom, I know how much it means to you to have everyone come to your house for the holidays..." and before I could continue, my mother said, "But I know that's not always possible." Wow! All I did was express understanding for what I knew to be her feelings! She responded with such unexpected grace! I explained how, this year, we wanted to host our little family at our home. She understood.

I believe that starting with a statement that demonstrated I understood her feelings was key to getting an even better response than I expected. She felt heard before she'd said a word. Feeling heard, she, in this case, responded with gracious acceptance of that year's change in plans.

OPTION TWO: CHANGE MY PERSPECTIVE

My friend, Emily, has many issues with her stubborn and domineering mother. She is working hard to sort out appropriate boundary issues in regard to their complicated relationship. One of the issues Emily brought up in a coaching session was whether or not to give her mother a ride to church. Emily also picks up four teenagers and takes them to church. Her mother lives closer to church than Emily does. Her mother still drives competently and is capable of driving herself. Emily believes that her mother's refusal to drive to church is just a ploy for control... to make Emily prove that her mother is important.

Emily wanted to tell her mother, "You can drive. I have all these kids I must also pick up. I'll meet you at the front door so you can still sit with us." It sounded logical and reasonable, if you didn't know the rest of the story.

I said, "Emily, one of the things you deeply hope for is to know that as your children mature—become adults—that you will still be important to them... that they'll love and appreciate you. Try to put yourself in the shoes of a 65 year old woman who lives alone. There are many other issues with her where you can set appropriate boundaries, but perhaps this issue is one where you can give your mother the convenience and reassurance that she appears to need."

Emily immediately agreed. She said, "You're right! This isn't the place to take a stand. If I make picking her up a control issue, she probably won't come to church. She thoroughly enjoys the church services. This is one time during the week when she gets out of the house, meets others, and enjoys being with us. I'll keep picking her up. It's a loving act of service that I can give her."

In this case, shifting Emily's perspective wiped out the resentment about picking up her mother for church each Sunday. Other issues with her mother may require different options.

ANOTHER REASON TO CHANGE YOUR PERSPECTIVE
If the reason for the resentment is because you've been expecting him or her to do something that can only be done for yourself, write down several possible steps that would assist you in taking responsibility for things that are within your control. You are not committing to do them, just writing them down.

For example: If you want more self-assurance, would a martial arts class or a journaling workshop appeal to you? If you feel tired of taking care of everyone else in the family so that no time is left for you, are you willing to give yourself 15 minutes every morning to meditate? Or read a novel you've been wishing you had time to read? Or end every day with a bubble bath? Or take a walk. Or hit a bucket of balls on your way home from work? Or join a sports league where you can get sweaty and be safely aggressive once a week?

If you want more financial stability, would purchasing a book such as Suze Orman's *9 Steps to Financial Freedom* get you started? If you feel burdened by debt but your partner isn't ready to join you in a strategic plan to get out of debt, perhaps you could read *How to Get Out of Debt and Stay Out of Debt and Live Comfortably* by Jerrold Mundis and begin implementing the simple steps outlined. Are you willing to set an intention for the financial condition you desire and commit to building your belief in its fulfillment?

If your marriage is feeling stale, could you plan a regular date with your honey? Ask for a regular date for a *Skilled Dialogue* to work out issues? Both take the Love Languages quiz online to see how you can increase the confidence you are both loved in the relationship?

(http://www.5lovelanguages.com/) Read ***Communication Elixers*** together?

OPTION THREE: SETTING A BOUNDARY

If the other person is not willing to change a hurtful behavior, or demonstrates repeatedly that he or she has no intention of following through with an agreement to change, and shifting your perspective just won't get the job done, then setting a boundary is the only option left to you. Boundary setting is to change how you relate to the issue. Boundaries change your behavior in relationship to the other person. A boundary is not to control the other person, but to eliminate resentment that is poisoning your health and the relationship. A boundary is to protect you from the abusive or thoughtless behavior of another.

The following is a list of possible ideas. All of them describe actions over which you have total control.

I will stop nagging about this issue. Nagging is trying to make the other person change, but it hasn't worked so far, so is unlikely to effect change in the future. I will give up the unrealistic expectation that he/she will change as a result of my nagging or just because I want him or her to change.

I will stop believing promises that are repeatedly broken, but believe the behavior rather than the words.

I will look for alternative, healthy ways to meet my need for peace.

I will release him or her to their own learning process, rather than demanding that he or she be in a place that is comfortable for me.

I will attend a Codependents Anonymous meeting at least three times to see what I can learn there.

I will purchase and read Melody Beattie's *Codependent No More* or Gay and Kathlyn Hendrick's *Conscious Loving* to build on my understanding of healthy relationships vs. codependency.

I will stop pretending that I am tolerant of a behavior or attitude that is intolerable to me. I will speak my truth respectfully.

I will stop enabling a behavior that is hurtful, such as buying booze for someone who drinks to excess.

I will no longer jeopardize my financial stability by bailing him out when he's in trouble.

Even if I am financially able, I will not rescue her from the consequences of her choices.

I will say "no" to invitations that I feel resentful about accepting. I will make an appointment with a counselor to help me see new options and get support for personal changes.

SUMMARY

I can think of a hundred different circumstances that may be the source of resentment in a relationship. The examples I've used only cover a few, but I hope they give you some ideas about how to proceed with your particular issues. If you are ready, choose one of those things and do it today, or put it on the calendar to do at a specific time.

"The only difference between rats and human beings is that human beings will go down cheese-less tunnels forever because they're more intent on proving to themselves that they're right than they are in finding and eating the cheese! (The cheese, in this case, is the elimination of resentment from your relationships.) When you do more of what hasn't been working, you not only fail to eliminate the problems in your life, you actually make things worse." *The Divorce Remedy* by Michele Weiner Davis, p. 94-95. Chapters 5 and 6 of *The Divorce Remedy* is full of ideas for different ways of doing things that effectively bring about healthy change.

The next chapter will list many more practical examples, both big and small, of sources of resentment and appropriate boundaries that will remove the cause of the resentment.

STIR THE POT

What relationship or resentment have you identified that needs your most immediate attention? Can you see the contribution you have made in creating or sustaining this issue...your part in the codependent dance? What options have you learned about here that you're willing to consider? Write them down. Imagine yourself following through with each one. What feelings surface in you as you imagine taking one of these steps? Do you need extra support as you "break the rules" by asking for a Skilled Dialogue, Changing your Perspective or Setting a Boundary?

Chapter 9: MORE EXAMPLES

So we've looked at codependency through the kaleidoscope, taking views from several different directions. This chapter will give you several more examples of how to respond to common situations in ways that will (1) prevent the buildup of resentment in you toward others, and (2) are healthy for both you and the other person in the relationship. Although it would be impossible to anticipate and represent every relationship situation here, I believe that these examples will offer ideas for solutions or strategies from which you may draw inspiration.

REVIEW

Recovery from codependency is *never* about controlling another person. The other half of a Velcro relationship will simply do whatever he or she will do. Given what he or she does, recovery is totally about assuming *appropriate* responsibility for myself, my welfare, my needs, or decisions which can only, with good mental health, be made by me. My job is to clearly, cleanly and *only* take responsibility for myself and leave the other person's responsibilities on the table for them to accept, or not.

A dependable clue that lets you know that a change in *you* is required is when, no matter how much you beg, nag, threaten or harass, the other person isn't changing *his or her* behavior. A second rock-solid clue is when the resentment inside of you is persistent and growing, infecting your wellbeing with unhappiness. Codependence is an entanglement of one person's irresponsibility toward others with another person's irresponsibility for herself or himself. The following are examples of possible ways for you to take appropriate responsibility for yourself, reducing or eliminating the resentment that damages your well-being and kills relationships.

DRIVING ISSUES

In the car: "Your driving is unsafe! I am a nervous wreck every time I have to ride with you. Did you read about the accident in the paper that happened because the driver was doing what you're doing? You need a traffic safety course."

Recovery: Apologize for the nagging and insults. Ask for a *Skilled Dialogue* where you can express your feelings respectfully. Take several minutes to plan the "I…" messages you will use. If you have co-operation, brainstorm a driving agreement. My late husband Jim and I agreed that the driver slows down or leaves more space between cars whenever the passenger requests it. The driving conditions *always* seem more dangerous from the passenger seat because the passenger has no control. Jim also agreed to move to the right lane of the freeway at least one mile before the desired exit. Thank you, Jim! (In this and other potentially "hot" topics, Jim and I frequently used the format for a *Skilled Dialogue*. Instructions for this powerful method of speaking and listening in order to find workable solutions is offered as a free download at www.nancylandrum.com)

One couple had an argument on the way to our workshop. They both arrived angry. He was speeding in order to arrive on time. She felt unsafe and asked him to slow down which he refused to do. His inner rule book was shouting to him, "It's rude to be late! Don't be late! Drive faster!" In a *Skilled Dialogue* he realized that his behavior was demonstrating that being on time to avoid others thinking badly of him was a higher priority than driving in such a way that his wife felt safe. The order of his priorities was not reflecting his true love for his wife. He gladly agreed that in the future he would slow down when she felt unsafe. That decision reassured his wife that her needs and their relationship were most important to him.

One wife asks to be let out to take a cab when her husband is reckless. For another couple, the wife always drives because she is so afraid of his driving. Do whatever works for the two of you without creating resentment for either one.

Recently a client caught herself berating her husband for his unsafe driving. She stopped, apologized, and quietly said, "I feel unsafe when you…" He reported that this message was so much easier to hear than the previous nagging. He willingly adjusted his driving behavior.

If you are uncomfortable, take full responsibility for your feelings. Without blaming, using the respectful speaking and listening skills taught in **Communication Elixirs**, try to work out a solution agreeable to both partners. If that doesn't work, then find a solution that takes care of your need to feel safe, allowing your partner to feel whatever feelings come up as a result of your *respectful* decision.

LAUNDRY ISSUES

Complaint: "He never turns his underwear or socks right side out before putting them in the laundry. I resent the extra work." Then leave them inside out. They wash just as clean that way. If it's important to him, he can turn them right side out before dressing.

One wife was talking about divorce because her husband didn't tri-fold the bath towels and hang them up after a shower with the labels facing to the back. There's no doubt that there were issues in this relationship other than how the towels were hung on the rack. But why not just cut the labels off?

Children ten or twelve years old are capable of learning how to do their own laundry. Whatever age your children are when you teach them, is certainly up to you. But after a child is taught how to manage the sorting and settings on the washer and dryer, and is expected to do his own laundry, the scene is ripe for a challenge.

If he complains that he has nothing clean to wear, allow him the reasonable consequence of wearing dirty clothes. Stepping in to remove the consequence is teaching him that he doesn't have to be responsible, even though he's been given this job to do on his own. It's not the time for a lecture. Let the consequence teach the lesson. Reasonable consequences are the very best teachers of responsibility. You might simply say, "Gosh, I'm sorry your laundry wasn't done!" and let it go.

When my adult son Steven came home to live, laundry became an issue between us. His dirty laundry would pile up in his small room until it smelled stinky. If up to him, the sheets on the bed would never be changed. I nagged. He promised. He didn't follow through. I berated and nagged some more. Finally I realized that my priority to have a reasonably clean home conflicted with his priority of doing whatever he wanted, which never included doing laundry.

He finally agreed to have his laundry done and room clean by 3 p.m. each Saturday. If it was not done by that time, I could, according to our agreement, do the job for him for the price of $10. The first few weeks when I calmly entered his room, gathered the laundry and returned everything to him clean, he was insulted, angry, and resentful. I was calm and happy. Each week he had the choice between doing it himself or paying me to do it. He never did the chore himself. The $10 per week meant that I could have my nails done every two weeks, a luxury we couldn't afford at that time. Eventually he became appreciative of this maid service and didn't resent paying for it. He always had a clean room and clean clothes to wear. My need for a clean, orderly home was met and I got to have my nails done. A win-win solution!

PARENTING CHALLENGES

Simple, age-appropriate consequences consistently delivered are a parent's best friends. It's simple to give a two-year-old a two minute time out in the corner for biting a playmate. Things get more complicated as children get older. One of the main reasons parents have a hard time enforcing consequences as children get older is because the consequence often involves inconvenience to the parent. As parents, we must accept that we assumed the responsibility of parenting this child until he is able responsibly to care for himself and let go of resentment when that inconveniences us. The following ideas work best when done matter-of-factly, without lectures, just a, "Sorry, but this is what happens when you…!" If you haven't already noticed, kids' behaviors change in response to action, (uncomfortable consequences) not lectures. So don't delude yourself with the belief that you are "doing something about the problem" if all you do is lecture. And, by the way, it's unrealistic to expect your child to appreciate your enforcing of consequences.

So when an eight year old won't get out of bed and get ready for school in the morning, put him to bed 30 minutes earlier that night. (This worked like magic to cure morning slowness and complaints with one of our kids.) If, as a ten year old, he forgets to put his sports uniform in the laundry, let him wear a dirty uniform to the game. If a twelve year old leaves her homework at home, rather than running it up to the school for her, allow her to get a lower grade for turning it in late. If a sixteen year old does not return home on time from an event where she was allowed to drive the car, after making sure she is safe and there was not a very good reason, refuse to let her drive anywhere for the next two weeks? Month? The inconvenience of being her chauffeur is worth the humiliation she will feel when she is escorted to necessary events by her parent. If a fourteen year old is using the computer for other than approved purposes, move the computer to the kitchen or family room where you can monitor his choices. And the "price" for getting a Facebook or other social media site is that you must have access. Monitor the site regularly. If she is running up a cell phone bill, either place the account in her name so she must pay the bill or service will be disconnected, confiscate the cell phone, or get her a pay-as-you-go cell phone.

One sixteen year old girl was allowed to wear her ratty cut-off jeans around the house, but expressly forbidden to wear them anywhere else. One cold morning her dad drove her to school wrapped in a blanket. When they arrived at school, she slithered out of the car, leaving the blanket, and hoped to get away without his noticing that she was wearing her very brief cut-offs. It didn't work.

He called to her, "Do you want to get back in the car so I can take you home to change? Or do you want me to pull you out of class to change when I come back with more appropriate clothes?" She yelled, "I'll be late!" and with a huff went into class hoping she had called his bluff.

Dad went home, got a pair of jeans, drove back to school, went to the office and had them call her out of class. The office staff said that this particular teacher hated interruptions to her class. Too bad! The daughter stomped into the office, grabbed her jeans from dad, and as she left, dad said, "Before you go back to class, bring me the cut-offs." He waited...and waited. Finally he called her out of class again, because, without the cut-offs in his hands, he couldn't be sure she'd changed. In a big huff, she came charging through the office door, handed her dad the cut-offs and went back to the additional consequence of a teacher who was very unhappy with her! Yay, dad!

No matter how inconvenient this was for the dad, he'd won an important battle with his trying-to-be-too-independent daughter. She demonstrated that she wasn't mature enough to make a wise decision about appropriate apparel. He demonstrated that she was important enough to him to enforce a reasonable boundary that was designed for her safety.

GIFT GIVING

My son Steven's ADHD condition combined with an undisciplined, drug addicted lifestyle meant that he was very hard on all his possessions. His brother told me once that he hated to give Steve a birthday or Christmas gift because it inevitably got lost or ruined. I shared with him the strategy I'd adopted to avoid this source of resentment. I only gave Steve things that I didn't care if he ruined. The consequence of Steve's irresponsibility meant that he never got gifts that were expensive or of good quality. From then on, both his brother and I could enjoy the pleasure of giving Steve a gift without the consequence *to us* of feeling resentment when it was ruined. Another option could have been to just give a card, or take him out for a meal, or bake a cake...all of which I sometimes did. I never gave him money, however. I did not want to finance his next drug fix.

The past few years I realized that I was feeling uncomfortable about giving expensive gifts to my grandchildren. They are always appreciative and have not ever acted entitled to such gifts. But two years ago I decided to make a change. In November I sent them a catalog from a well-known charity. From the catalog they each chose a gift that would benefit a child in a part of the world where people are desperately poor and genuinely in need of help. They notified me of their choices by December 1st.

In the name of one grandchild, I ordered a goat and two chickens to provide milk and eggs as well as a means to develop self-sustaining assets for a needy family. In the name of the other grandchild, I ordered a bicycle so that a girl could travel to and from her school more safely. The charity sent my grandchildren beautiful "Thank you" acknowledgements in time for Christmas, as did I. I got the pleasure of giving gifts that benefitted truly needy children as well as contributing to my grandchildren's awareness of those who live far below their American middle-class standard. For now, this is my Christmas policy for them. I continue to give them personal gifts on their birthdays.

HEALTH AND GROOMING ISSUES

One acquaintance regularly harassed her husband about his smoking habit. It, predictably, created a wall of resentment between them. She wasn't prepared to leave him over this issue. She eventually chose a change in perspective. She decided that the resentment was creating as much poison between them as the cigarette smoke. He agreed to only smoke outside. She dropped her nagging about it, while hoping that he will one day choose to quit for his own well-being.

Another friend was dismayed by the way her husband dressed when they went shopping together. In her words, he looked slovenly, unkempt, like a tramp. It embarrassed her. All it took in this case was a *Skilled Dialogue* sharing how she felt in order to resolve the issue. He can dress comfortably, even sloppily around the house, but when he goes out with her he smartens himself up. He wants her to feel proud to be with him. What others think of him doesn't matter to him, but what *she* thinks of him, does.

SPECIAL OCCASIONS

I've often heard this complaint which seems more common from women, rather than men although it may be true from either gender:

"I resent the way he forgets special occasions. He never remembers my birthday or even his mother on Mother's Day. He bought me a toaster for Christmas! I feel angry when I have to remind him of special occasions. If he loved me, he would be more aware of these things."

Recovery is accepting that it is not your responsibility to monitor someone else's relationship with his (or her) family. What he does or doesn't do with his mother on Mother's Day is none of your business. That is between him and his mother. If you choose to, you may send her a card representative of *your own* relationship with her. Or, if he asks you, you may, as a favor to him, buy a card for him to give his mother.

A general tip that works best in most relationships is that each person deals with any issues stemming from his or her own family. If corrections or adjustments or boundaries must be set, he does it when it involves his family. She takes care of issues having to do with her family. Trying to settle issues with each other's families opens the door for severe judgment on the non-family member and the possibility of a relationship triangle forming which is always damaging to everyone involved. A relationship triangle is, for instance, her trying to stop his dad from criticizing him, him resenting her getting between him and his dad, the dad being mad at her for interfering and also judging his son as a wimp for allowing her to speak for him. It's best for each to deal with his or her own family's issues.

It's unwise to measure love based on whether or not your gift expectations have been met. It would be wise, however, to ask for a *Skilled Dialogue* to respectfully share your feelings about this issue and, if your partner is open to this, brainstorm some practical solutions such as:

- Give him a list of stores from which you would welcome gift certificates.
- Ask if you can make a shopping date with him when an occasion approaches.
- Agree on an amount of money you can spend on yourself for special occasions.
- Ask if it's O.K. to write a reminder in his date book with suggestions of things you would like.

- Initiate a discussion of love languages. Tell him your feelings when you are remembered with a gift.
- Determine to positively reinforce with gratitude every remembrance or expression of love that is offered.

BOSSINESS OR NAGGING

This complaint seems to be more common coming from men: "She is so bossy. She is constantly telling me what to do. I feel like a little boy being harassed by his mother. She is so afraid I won't complete a project that she nags me about it. In reaction, I procrastinate even more to punish her."

- Again, recovery begins with a *Skilled Dialogue* where feelings can be *respectfully* shared. The "nag-ee" may open by confessing his tactic of deliberate procrastination and apologize for practicing that underhanded method of communication.
- When both persons have shared feelings without blame or accusations, brainstorm some solutions along the line of:
    - o She agrees to ask once and then drop it unless choosing to bring up the issue respectfully again in another *Skilled Dialogue.*
    - o He agrees to give a reasonable date by which project will be completed. He is accountable to keep his word.
    - o If unforeseen events require postponement, he talks about them with her, and sets a new date for which he is responsible.
    - o If several postponements occur, husband acknowledges his responsibility for the consequence of undermining her trust in his word and accepts responsibility for the time and effort it will take to regain her trust. Back to *Skilled Dialogues.*
    - o If necessary, agree on a date beyond which she will step in to do the project without interference, or someone will be hired to complete it without *any* complaint from him.

MONEY ISSUES

Although this complaint may come from males or females, this example identifies a man as the one complaining: "She never balances the checkbook! She won't stick to a budget! The bills aren't paid on time and our credit rating is being damaged. We were turned down for a lower interest mortgage because of our poor credit rating. I resent being the victim of her financial irresponsibility!"

For some reason, most of us are so vulnerable when it comes to money issues. We often have family of origin issues underneath the surface issue of overspending or extreme frugality. It would probably be helpful to explore what money means to each person. What do I need from a perfect credit rating besides a lower interest loan? What does the freedom to buy things represent? Why is it such an emotionally threatening issue? It will be easier to work out a solution that meets both person's needs if you have a compassionate understanding of what money represents to each.

Possible solutions:

The complainer takes over the bill paying to make sure bills are paid on time, thus protecting your credit rating. The complainer may also, based on the past six months of spending records, work out monthly averages for each category. This based-on-reality-report may show clearly that more money is being spent than is coming in each month. Let the reality do the educating. Set a date for a *Skilled Dialogue* after you've each had a chance to look at this reality check.

Use an envelope method of paying for household expenses. Each pay period, a set amount of cash goes into the grocery envelope, the clothing envelope, the gas envelope, etc. It's gone when it's gone. Jim and I found that we each needed an allowance—money for which we didn't have to answer to each other. We also set aside a "couple allowance" every week—money with which we do things together. During our worst financial time, the personal weekly allowance was $5 each and the couple (date) allowance was $20. As our financial condition became better, our allowances became more generous.

A date is set for paying bills together, or one person pays them and gives a report to the other so both know where the account stands.

The man (in this case) must agree not to nag, insult, or blame, and the woman consents to stay within the agreed-upon limits. Both understand that keeping their agreements will eliminate conflict and rebuild trust. Terms can be renegotiated if either feels the need.

If these options don't work, do what you would do if you wanted to learn how to dance or do wood-working . . . take lessons! Interview several financial planners describing what you need. Ask how he or she might support you in learning. Hire the one with whom you are the most comfortable. Or take an adult education class together.

ADVANCED RECOVERY

Advanced recovery from codependency is learning to apply these concepts of shared responsibility to feelings as well as behaviors. Each person is not only individually responsible for the *behaviors* chosen, but also the *feelings* felt or, at the least, how the feelings are managed. One of my greatest challenges as a relationship coach is to weed out "she/he makes me feel" from a person's speech pattern. As a culture we seem to support the notion that another person is responsible for how I feel— therefore, my feelings are that person's fault. In addition, one national pass-time is trying to guess what another person is thinking or feeling so an appropriate response can be planned. I confess I frequently catch myself at this fruitless game, even yet.

Inner thought: "He said he's glad to take me to the doctor and be with me during this painful test, but I don't know if he really means it. What if he really doesn't want to go and will be resentful about being there? I think I'll just drive myself to make sure. But I'm frightened of the test and want him to be with me. I wish he would express himself more *emphatically* so I could be sure he means it."

Recovery: None of us can read another person's mind. Each person is responsible to speak his or her own truth. I am responsible to tell my partner that I want his support while going through the test. My partner is responsible to tell the truth about whether or not he wants to be there or can be there. I must assume my partner is telling the truth. I act on what I've been told. I do not hold myself responsible for guessing what is true for my partner. If what is said is not true, the one telling an untruth must deal with the consequence of that deceit.

It is impossible to over-emphasize the importance of each person being responsible to tell the truth—respectfully and as kindly as possible, but the truth. Healthy relationships will only be built on the truth.

ACCOUNTABILITY

One of my teachers often said that you can count on someone behaving now the way she has in the past unless a different behavior has been demonstrated, repeatedly, over a significant period of time. A concept that goes hand in hand with that one is to evaluate another's behavior, not their words. "Words are cheap," as the saying goes. Behavior is what determines whether a person is trustworthy or not, particularly the behavior of keeping one's agreements.

In a family night meeting at a drug rehab facility, the leader asked, "Are love and trust synonymous? Is trust always a part of loving someone?"

That night I heard many horror stories from parents and others who love an addict… stories of loving that addict so much that they sacrificed a lot to try to help that addict be healthy. Then, time and again, the excruciating pain of being tricked, robbed, abused, and betrayed by a person who did not keep his or her word. Some parents expressed the horror and grief of having to call in the police when their child was physically abusive or refused to leave the premises when asked.

Love is entirely separate from trust. Love just is… it's a choice, or even an instinct, to love someone. But trust can only *safely* and *accurately* be based on that person's behavior…his track record of keeping agreements, behaving respectfully and responsibly. Trust must be earned, and re-earned if trust has been broken.

The classic codependent symptom is to love someone so much, to want the relationship to work so much, that trust is given when a person hasn't demonstrated the quality of trustworthiness. Codependents tend to overlook or explain away "red flags" that often show up early in a relationship. Loving someone, means we *want* to believe the best of him.

Loving someone often translates into reluctance to believe, or denial of, the evidence that she is untrustworthy.

SUMMARY

Codependence has many faces. Codependence shows up in a variety of ways and circumstances. Recovery from codependence in a relationship requires the making and keeping of agreements. If one person is not ready to keep his or her part of the agreement, then a boundary is needed to protect the other person in the relationship. Recovery is a process of eliminating resentment by holding the other accountable for his or her behavior with appropriate consequences if agreements are broken. Recovery from codependent feelings and behaviors is hard work, but ultimately much easier than constantly feeling frustration, resentment and exhaustion from functioning in relationship with someone who is not responsible.

I consider every situation or relationship in which I've had to disconnect from disempowering codependence and establish a boundary, a personal call to growth. No one has challenged me more than those I love the most. From that perspective, my two husbands and two sons have been my greatest teachers and deserve, and receive, my heart-felt appreciation. Because of lessons learned in relationship with them, I am a better, more conscious, stronger and more empathic person.

STIR THE POT: Evaluating the Examples

As you read through the variety of examples given in this chapter, did your experience resonate with some of the scenarios? Which ones? Do you tend to trust others, even when red flags are present, because it's easier than dealing with the potential issues up front? Do you want to trust someone so badly that you leave yourself vulnerable to his lies, excuses, abuse or betrayal? Do you cling to the belief that she should change her behavior because, after all, she's in the wrong, rather than taking appropriate steps to protect yourself? Does the whole idea of setting self-protective boundaries repulse you? Why? Do you unrealistically expect others to act responsibly toward you so that you don't have to set appropriate boundaries? Is there one example or issue or relationship that you are ready to address using the options outlined in Chapter 8?

Chapter 10: THE VOICE

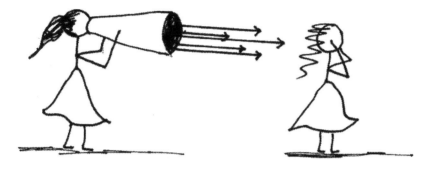

"The rules" as introduced in Chapter 7, are things like: don't talk back, be nice, don't question authority, stay quiet, believe what you're told, do what you're asked to do without argument, go along to get along, don't rock the boat, avoid confrontation at all costs, suck it up, don't complain, say "yes" because it's the right or expected thing to do, cooperation is owed to another, boys will be boys, women are just like that, that's just the way things are.

Well-meaning persons of authority taught us "the rules" to help us fit into a family or cultural system that made sense at that time. We may also have adopted rules that, as a child, helped us navigate an environment that was not safe. There's no doubt that making changes in relationship to a loved one, valued friend, or in a working environment will often bring to the surface every insecurity, fear and old rule that lives buried within.

Contemplating the possibility of breaking "the rules" may bring up fear-based questions like these: What if he won't love me anymore? What if I lose my job? What if she gets mad at me? What if he leaves me? How will I support myself? How can I possibly challenge my mother? My dad? Will the family reject me if I don't attend the wedding, baby shower, or holiday celebration? Will *they* think I'm mean? Would I be bad if I …? What if he's disappointed in me? Am I wrong to want to…?

Am I selfish to want …? Is it unrealistic to insist on being treated with respect? But what will happen to him/her if I don't help? How can I call myself a good friend, parent, partner if I allow her to suffer these awful consequences? If I choose to *not* help, does that mean I'm unloving? Stingy? Selfish?

THE VOICE

If these "rules" were not so deeply embedded in our psyches, recovery from codependency would be easy. But our brains love rules. Rules bring order out of what would otherwise be chaos. The brain has a reminder mechanism for helping us stick to whatever rules were embedded. In psychology this reminder mechanism has been labeled various things such as the internalized parent, the superego, or the inner critic. I like to call it The Voice, a term taken from the writings of Geneen Roth, author of *Women, Food and God*.

The Voice has our best interests at heart. The Voice doesn't want us to get into trouble. The Voice wants us to be "good." The Voice reminds us to brush our teeth so we don't get cavities. The Voice may say, "One glass of wine is enough," or "Remember to call Mom today." The Voice doesn't know a good habit from a bad habit…a good rule from a harmful one. It only knows that doing its job means keeping us on the straight and narrow track of "the rules." When the habits embedded in our brains are healthy, The Voice helps us maintain those habits. When the habits embedded are not so healthy, The Voice still fights to keep us practicing those habits because that is The Voice's job. It isn't discriminating. It tries to uphold all habits without passing judgment, without question, without evaluation.

I'm not a brain expert, and don't know the various parts and their names and functions, so I'm going to keep it simple. I'm calling it Consciousness when we can use our brain to look at a relationship or circumstance objectively and then evaluate what is and what isn't working.

So, for instance, the Conscious part decides, "I'm tired of attending family gatherings where Uncle Charlie drinks too much and becomes abusive. I'm no longer willing to spend a precious day off enduring such craziness. I will see the other members of my family at other times, but no longer attend gatherings when Uncle Charlie will be there."

That decision is perceived as a call to action for The Voice. The Voice will say, "You can't do that! They will all be upset with you. They will think you're stuck up…too good for the family. What if Uncle Charlie punishes the rest of the family because you don't show up? Just go with the flow. You're selfish to upset everyone just so you won't have to put up with Uncle Charlie. Besides, don't you love him? He's really old and kind of pathetic. You should have more compassion."

Do you hear all the "rules" that The Voice is trying to enforce? The Conscious decision to protect yourself from Uncle Charlie's abusive behavior is an attempt to establish a new rule. The new rule says, "My days off and times with my family are important enough that I want them to be pleasant. I am not willing anymore to support Uncle Charlie's drinking by passively putting up with it. This new rule is healthy for me, and ultimately healthy for Uncle Charlie, as well."

Recovery from codependency and courageously taking steps to weed resentment and dysfunction out of your relationships requires that the Conscious part of you be willing to examine and evaluate "the rules." You then make a deliberate, aware choice about whether or not a particular rule, or cluster of rules, is healthy for you. If you decide that "the rule" needs to be replaced with a new, more self-honoring, and in the context of this book, less codependent rule, you must be prepared to push past the predictable protests from The Voice. The new self-respectful rule and accompanying behavior will have to be practiced several times, becoming a new habit, before The Voice will support the new and stop pressuring you to obey the old.

WHISPERS

If The Voice played fair and spoke at a normal volume, it would be easy to recognize it and evaluate its message. But The Voice is sneaky. It loves to hide just below the level of our conscious awareness. When you first try to identify The Voice, you have to go on a hunt, searching for clues. Just as though you are a tracker trying to find a rogue tiger that's been attacking innocent people, you look for evidence that The Voice has been in the area, stalking you.

The footprints and broken twigs that The Voice leaves behind are feelings such as shame, guilt, embarrassment, self-doubt, self-judgment, exhaustion, sadness, depression, and disappointment in yourself. Another emotion may be determination to be better or do it right next time so that he, she, or *everyone* will be happy with you. And, of course, somewhere in the murkiness, you'll also find the classic codependent feeling of *resentment*...or even rage.

TURNING UP THE VOLUME

The next step is to expose The Voice...the instigator of these feelings. You do that by asking yourself questions like these: What am I telling myself? What accusations are being used as whips with which to beat myself up? What old rules am I hearing? What childhood belief do I think I still must abide by? What names am I calling myself? What do I think I have to do to be loved? Accepted? Safe? Good?

The Voice *sounds* like your voice...or the voice of your mother or father or some revered person of authority...even God. But The Voice is separate from you. It is The Voice of the Enforcer of the Rules listed in the first paragraph of this chapter. So even though it sounds like your voice, it is helpful to separate yourself from it by calling it The Voice. To assist you in doing that, change the wording of your questions. Ask, "What is The Voice telling me? What accusations is The Voice using to beat me up? What old rules is The Voice trying to enforce? What old, dysfunctional belief is The Voice using to whip me? What names is The Voice calling me? What does The Voice want me to do in order to be loved?"

Just as the most abusive and brutal dictators can only maintain power by instilling overpowering fear in their citizens, The Voice rules with crippling fear. As introduced in Chapter 6, the fear targets two vulnerable areas. The first fear is that someone I care about can't handle the painful consequences of his or her behavior. Or, a subset of that fear is that *I* can't handle seeing that loved one suffer. The first fear is mostly camouflage for the *real* fear. The *real* fear is that I will be, or be thought of by others as, a bad, heartless and cruel person if I allow someone for whom I care to suffer the painful consequences of his or her behavior. The *real* fear is of breaking the rules…the beliefs… that have governed my life since childhood.

EXAMPLE ONE

Jane's mom and dad were solid, responsible people who took the job of parenting five children seriously. There was never a question about how devoted they were to their family. Jane knew that her parents were there for her, no questions asked.

Jane married and had three children with a man who became an alcoholic. Jane was there for her children in ways that their father wasn't. He was too immersed in drink to be emotionally available to his children. His focus was feeding his addiction, rather than being a good father for his kids.

If there had been no children, Jane may have left him. But, for the sake of the children, according to her rule book, she stayed and cared for their father. She put up with his rages, his efforts to control and shame her. He didn't want her to have a job that would identify her as his intellectual equal, so she cleaned houses to keep food on the table for their children. She stuck it out. She demonstrated admirable qualities of commitment, hard work and fortitude all while being the emotional anchor for their three growing children. She crossed the finish line as a victorious survivor when her husband suffered from, and ultimately succumbed to end-stage alcoholism and died.

Chuck, a knight in shining armor, arrived on the scene a year or two later. He rescued her from her house-cleaning job, believed in her abilities, cheered her on as she took on a responsible job with a local firm and earned regular promotions. He welcomed her and her three pre-teens into his comfortable home. Becoming an instant father figure to half-grown children was challenging. He thought that the children were too dependent on Jane…that she did too much for them, put up with what he saw as their laziness and helped them when he thought they didn't really need help. Jane didn't appreciate his point of view. The children resisted his authority. He comforted himself with the expectation that it would only be a few years until they were grown and out of the house. After all, he'd been supporting himself and living independently since the age of eighteen. For a while, it looked like that plan was working.

The daughter married and had a baby. But then her marriage hit a rough patch and Jane welcomed her back home. A son returned from a tour in the military with symptoms of post-traumatic stress disorder (PTSD) and he, too, moved back in with them. Chuck was relieved when the third child appeared to be thriving in his chosen profession and in no danger of coming home. But the on-going stress of adult children and a baby in the house pushed Chuck's coping to the limit and burdened the marriage. They came to me for help.

Better communication skills helped. Chuck gradually learned to replace his judgmental declarations with gentler methods of *Speaking to be Heard*. He worked at really *Listening to Understand* Jane's point of view. Jane stretched to speak her truth in *Skilled Dialogues*, rather than running from the conflicts. (These skills are taught in **Communication Elixers**, the second book in the **Love Potions** series.)

These steps were important, but the reinforcing of their marriage may not have been possible without Jane's willingness to explore the concepts of codependency. She began to examine the parenting rules she'd adopted from her parents. Her internalized interpretation was that the parents *always* support the children…that the children *always* have a safe harbor to which to return if the storms of life get too hard for them. She examined what it was she was teaching her adult children by continuing to cook, clean and house them without charging room and board. She courageously looked at what she was modeling for them as a wife whose marriage was floundering because of her excessive commitment to her children. The rules, the basis for her behavior choices, were exposed.

Jane also heard The Voice telling her that she would be a bad mother if she didn't "support" her children in their times of need. She began to redefine what it meant to be a good mother to adult children. She eventually formulated a new rule: a good mother of adult children supports them in supporting themselves. A good mother nudges them out of the nest to gain the confidence to fly on their own. A good mother helps a son suffering from PDSD to find available support services that can more objectively help him recover. A good mother encourages the growth of her child's self-esteem by encouraging her to learn relationship skills that will restore her marriage. A good mother knows that there is a time to withdraw excessive care-taking so that her children recognize their own strengths and learn appropriate adult life-lessons.

The day came when, by using the Problem Solving Worksheet taught in *Savory Safeguards*, they hammered out a strategy to gently, but firmly, remove both adult children from the umbrella of enabling, excessive protection and force them to be appropriately independent. At the same time, Chuck and Jane began making plans for the balance of their life together. They took a good look at their finances and decided to move to an area where the cost of living is less so they could adequately save for their retirement years. For the first time, Chuck felt as though he had a voice in their marriage. Jane's perception of herself as a good mother remained the same, but with a new understanding of what that meant in relationship to adult children. Their marriage was infused with new hope and renewed energy.

EXAMPLE TWO
Mary thought that she and John were exclusively dating each other and on their way to a permanent relationship. When Mary and John were engaged, she discovered that he had been unfaithful to her when they were dating. He excused this behavior by saying they weren't committed to each other when the unfaithfulness occurred. She accepted his explanation, and let the issue go.

A few years later, they had their first child. John was overwhelmed with a level of responsibility for which he didn't feel prepared. He left Mary and their daughter for more than a year. During that time, although they hadn't divorced, he was again, unfaithful. He eventually realized that Mary was the woman he wanted. He begged forgiveness. Mary took him back.

They had two more children. John started a cabinet making business that, for a while, flourished, but required 60-80 hour work weeks. Mary was left to assume almost full care of the children…in essence, a single mom. John was an excellent designer and builder, but as the business grew, John's weakness as a manager was exposed. He kept the struggles a secret from Mary, so when he declared bankruptcy, it was a surprise to her. Again, she coped and they moved on.

Several years later he, again, started a cabinet making business, believing that, this time, he could make it work. As the business grew, and paperwork piled up, Mary suggested that John hire her best friend, Lucy, to manage the office. Lucy praised John for his beautiful designs and gorgeous cabinetry. By this time, Mary had worked several years managing a retail business. She kept pointing out the areas of John's weakness, managing his employees. She was trying to help him choose options that would strengthen his business. He heard it as criticism. He began a secret affair with Lucy. The affair necessitated multiple lies, of course. And, in addition, this business, also, began to fail under the weight of poor management. John lied to Mary about the severity of the business problems, as well. The affair was eventually exposed and bankruptcy was again declared.

Although Mary was furious and feeling betrayed by all the lies, as well as the affair, she was determined to see this marriage through. Her parents had divorced when she was young. She had vowed that she would never inflict the pain of divorce on her children that she experienced with her parents' divorce. The Voice was insisting that she stay and obey her vow (rule). Again, she worked her way through the emotional morass, accepted John's abject apologies, believed his promises, and did her best to move on. He got a new job across the country; they moved; and she found work.

They began to try to dig themselves out of the mess, believing they were making a new start. Only this time, she just couldn't get past the hurt and anger, as she had done before. She repeatedly lashed out at John, berating him for all the lies, all the betrayals. This last affair and business failure triggered an almost daily rehearsal of all the previous lies that she thought she had forgiven and left behind. Long-buried feelings were erupting like a molten volcano. She was drowning in anger and bitterness. Mary knew she could not survive even one more lie…one more betrayal. John knew he was to blame, but wondered how much longer he could bear the constant, corrosive attacks. They both knew they needed help. They could not keep doing their marriage as usual and expect it to survive.

We began working together using the affair recovery process outlined in Dave Carder's book and workbook titled *Torn Asunder: Recovering From an Extramarital Affair*. Mr. Carder assimilates a lifetime of experience helping couples either rebuild a healthy marriage from the ashes of betrayal, or work through the issues in such a way that the baggage of the patterns that erupted in an affair would not follow them into future relationships. Through a series of explorations and dialogues, he ruthlessly leads a couple to look with clear eyes at the elements that make a marriage susceptible to infidelity. John and Mary tracked the ups and downs of their twenty-six year relationship. They identified the stress points that resulted in John's lying about the business and beginning an affair. They dug into their family-of-origin histories, since the pattern of infidelity runs in families, just as does abuse, addictions and other dysfunctional behaviors. They agreed on a two week period where Mary could ask any question she wanted to ask and expect a totally truthful answer from John. After those two weeks, she agreed to stop the questions.

There's a lot more to the process as outlined by Dave Carder, but to describe it briefly, it's a process that exposed every hidden, unconscious pattern in both John and Mary so that they could see how their weaknesses combined to create the reality of their fragile marriage. John's lies and affairs were easy targets. We all agree that there's no excuse for his behaviors. However, Mary's pattern of compliance with his excessive work hours, lack of involved parenting, and determination to keep the marriage together at all costs also contributed to the repetition of dysfunctional patterns. Her inability to move beyond the most recent offenses were a signal that her need for trust and security were finally louder voices within her than The Voice who insisted she just keep coping with things the way they had been. She knew things had to change in the marriage or she couldn't stay.

Both John and Mary deeply wanted to rebuild their marriage, stronger, safer, and more emotionally intimate than they'd ever had in the past. They committed themselves to the process outlined in *Torn Asunder*. In addition, I began teaching them the communication skills that are the backbone of my work. They took the *Defective Communication Tools Inventory* shared in **Communication Elixirs** (and available as a free download at www.NancyLandrum.com) They saw how their methods of speaking and their inability to really hear each other contributed to the breakdown of emotional safety between them. John and Mary began learning how to have a *Skilled Dialogue* where each could speak truth *respectfully* and both be heard with *empathy*.

The final chapter about their marriage has not, as yet, been written. I have high hopes for them, based on what I can see of their commitment to examine, repair and rebuild their marriage with new information and skills. In this case, the voices in Mary's head that were shouting, "I can't take it anymore! This marriage has to change! I can't risk being betrayed again!" finally overcame The Voice that insisted she do whatever she had to in order to preserve the marriage's status quo.

EXAMPLE THREE
Overcoming outdated rules enforced by The Voice does not always mean the relationship is healed the way it was in the case of Chuck and Jane, and as I hope it will be with John and Mary. Kristen was reared in a home where religion was used to control, abuse and terrorize. She could hardly wait to escape the dictatorial, rigid control of her father. Consequently she fell for the first man who seemed to offer her the love and caring for which she longed. When she married him, and left the faith of her childhood, her father disowned her. She could not return to her family unless she was willing to embrace their religion. She was on her own.

When Kristen's first husband revealed himself as a drug addict and felon, she left that relationship with their son in tow. The next marriage was to a man who was verbally abusive. With him, she gave birth to two more children. She also began exploring the source of her relationship patterns. She is an insatiable reader, reading one book after another as a way of educating herself about herself. She began exploring a personal relationship with God and found a church that helped her know God as loving and forgiving. Although she is not in contact with her parents, she went through a process of deeply forgiving them and releasing whatever blame she held against them for the religious abuse that thrust her on this journey. Eventually, the second marriage ended, as well.

Kristen was very cautious about dating. In time, she dated a man who treated her extremely well in comparison to her father and previous husbands. Dan was fun. He creatively planned great activities for herself and her children. She noticed that he liked things done his way. He wanted his opinions heard and agreed with. She was a good listener and didn't really notice that he wasn't listening to her. She accommodated his preferences because, after all, they were so much more reasonable than being physically or verbally abused. They married.

Over time, issues between him and her children surfaced. Dan wanted control. He was certain that his opinions about how to handle pre-teens were better than the way Kristen was parenting. She eventually noticed that he wanted her support in working long hours, having several drinks when arriving home, and going to bed far later than she could afford to stay up. But when she said she needed more attention from him, or that his habit of being chronically late was annoying, she was being "unreasonable and unloving." They sought help from one counselor after another, all of whom suggested his priority of excessive working and drinking was damaging to their relationship. He insisted on leaving each of the counselors when his perspective was not supported.

After working with them for several months, I suggested Kristen read *Emotional Vampires: Dealing with People Who Drain You Dry* by Albert J. Bernstein, Ph.D. (a great book for codependents!). In this book, Dr. Bernstein describes the characteristics of narcissists and other extreme personality types and how to protect oneself from being their victim. The light bulbs went on. Her current husband was firmly stuck in a pattern of "I want what I want and what you want doesn't matter to me." Rather than blaming herself for choosing yet another, abusive man, Kristen recognized that she had, over time, as she had become emotionally healthier, chosen lesser, more subtle forms of abuse.

They parted amicably, he believing that she was unreasonable, she accepting responsibility for choosing unwisely and determined to continue her journey of in-depth education and healing. She went on to read Dr. Henry Cloud's book, *Necessary Endings: The Employees, Businesses, and Relationships That All of Us Have to Give Up in Order to Move Forward*. She is working hard to eradicate her assumption that she doesn't deserve respect. She is making changes in many of her relationships that evidence her new beliefs that she *is* deserving of respectful, appropriate attention, loyalty and love. She is quieting The Voice that told her she had to take what she could get, that she was damaged, that it was "her job" to save the marriage, that she was destined to repeat mistakes. With ongoing education and courage, she is establishing new beliefs that support new patterns in healthier relationships.

A PROFESSIONAL RELATIONSHIP EXAMPLE

Sharon was starting a new business. She needed help knowing how to maximize her business via on-line marketing. She hired Joan, a business coach she met at a networking meeting. They worked together for several months, during which Sharon learned a lot from Joan. Sharon often felt overwhelmed and intimidated by Joan's knowledge. Over time she felt inadequate, unable to move forward without Joan's coaching, and obligated to follow her instructions.

A couple of times during those months, Joan "went off" on Sharon, obviously angry with her about something. Sharon listened carefully, even asked questions, but couldn't decipher what she had done that triggered Joan's anger. When the tirades ended, they went back to work as though nothing had happened. Sharon felt cautious about continuing her relationship with Joan, but didn't know how to find a replacement for her expertise. Also, Joan had designed several support services that kept Sharon's business dependent on her management.

Due to some unrelated circumstances, there were a few months in a row when Sharon and Joan had little contact. The "break" allowed Sharon time to thoroughly think through the direction she wanted to take her business, the kind of business relationships she wanted to experience, and the qualities she wanted to be characteristic of her life. She decided that her main goal was to experience more love, joy and peace in her life. That intention, among other things, meant working with persons with whom navigating differences would be easy, without excessive drama. She also decided that it was time to trust that whatever she or her business needs, would be provided. It was time to reject the pressure Sharon felt to do things Joan's way.

Sharon carefully thought through how to approach Joan. Sharon was genuinely grateful for all she had learned from Joan, and expressed that appreciation generously. When Sharon shared her decision to make a change, being careful to not lay blame, Joan blew up again. This time, rather than feeling embarrassed and bewildered, Sharon just felt detached. She felt so detached that the only thought going through her head was, "I'm through with this relationship! I will not work with anyone who behaves like this!" Sharon followed up the phone conversation with an email severing their working relationship.

It was a leap of faith, as letting Joan go left a vacancy of skills that Sharon needed. Sharon chose to no longer listen to The Voice that told her she couldn't manage her business without Joan's help…that somehow it was her failure that triggered Joan's behavior. Sharon chose to believe that she could find the help she needed from persons who would treat her with respect and be in closer alignment with her goals. It took several weeks to find, interview and choose replacements to do the services that Joan had previously managed. It was such a relief, however, to be disconnected from the pressure of Joan's pushing style, and be free from the threat of another tirade. Sharon found she was able to easily move forward with more love for herself, more joy in her business and a much greater degree of peace than she had experienced in a long time.

SUMMARY

We all have some version of The Voice within. The Voice is useful in maintaining habits of thought and behavior that are for our good. But a higher, more conscious part of us must be in charge of evaluating relationships that are challenging and deciding on appropriate boundaries so that we can move forward with dignity and strength. When an appropriate boundary is established in a once unhealthy dynamic, the boundary will be in the best interests of both parties. The other party may not like or appreciate the change in the dynamic between the two of you, but will, nevertheless, benefit from your disconnection from codependency in the relationship. The Voice will eventually support the new, healthier "rules."

STIR THE POT: Growing Beyond The Voice

What childhood rules still dictate your behavior in ways that "cost you?" What are some examples? What do you hear The Voice saying to you when you go against some family rule or societal dictate? Do you have an example of listening to your own inner knowing, making a choice that was contrary to The Voice, and being satisfied with the result? Following your inner knowing, did you make a choice in the past for which The Voice still tortures you? Are you currently in a relationship with a partner, child, or employer where you consistently are expected to pick up the slack or rescue another's irresponsibility? What is The Voice telling you about that situation? Is The Voice supporting you or supporting the status quo? Are you ready to think about a supportive change?

Chapter 11: THE LAST CHAPTER

Steven continued to be my most valuable resource in "recovering" from co-dependent behavior. He consistently exposed layer after layer of mixed motives, faulty beliefs, and dysfunctional, irrational and egotistic needs in me. Thanks to his faithful "teaching," after a lot of noise, and even more pain, I eventually learned to set reasonable boundaries to keep myself from playing the role of a victim. I learned how to make decisions honoring *myself* that also honored him—his ability to make his own choices and experience the consequences, pleasant or not, from those choices. After many years of struggling with the sticky Velcro of our relationship, Steve and I both broke free, allowing us the hard won, sweet pleasure of just loving each other without hidden agendas and mutual manipulation.

About three months before he died, Steve decided that the only way he could die with self-respect was to die clean. He confessed to me that he had continued to "use" during the two previous years he'd been living with us due to his severely enlarged heart. He asked my forgiveness. I gave it to him wholeheartedly.

In a pattern of typical denial, I had blamed his erratic behavior on his attention deficit disorder and hyperactivity. My husband Jim had once tried to gently suggest that he still might be using drugs, but I refused to consider that possibility. It was beyond reason that someone dying from drug use would continue to use drugs. Addiction is not rational. Addiction has a life of its own that is entirely disconnected from health or relationship realities.

The night of Steve's confession, I was stunned. The following day I walked on the beach and wandered around a mall for an entire day, feeling like a sleep walker. The past two years had been so very hard. It was so challenging to live with Steve. I'd left a new job and devoted most of my energy to finding him the medical and psychological help he needed. My choices were based on the assumption that he would stay clean while under our roof and accepting our help. In spite of genuinely forgiving him, I felt betrayed. I was livid. I felt used. I took a few days to process all the volcanic feelings that erupted. By the end of that week, I crafted a contract that Steven could either agree to or move out. I would not be a willing, conscious participant in his addiction, even though he was near death. (Note: Forgiveness is separate from boundary setting. One can love and forgive a person while still finding it necessary to set a boundary to protect one's own wellbeing.)

I showed him the contract. He was angry. He thought I was assuming responsibility for his sobriety. He thought forgiving him meant that I would also trust him to remain clean for the remainder of his life. I assured him that I was only, finally, taking appropriate responsibility for what happened in my home, under my roof…for my own welfare. I was only putting in writing what he had already agreed to do, with some consequences if he didn't follow through.

The main points of the contract were these:

1. Every day that he was well enough, he would attend one meeting that supported his sobriety. That could be a Narcotics Anonymous meeting, attending church with his sober friend, or attending a session with the counselor with whom he was working.

2. If he was not well enough to go to one of these meetings, then he was too sick to hang out in the garage of the addict across the street or do anything else with anyone else.

3. All drug paraphernalia would be disposed of immediately and no drugs would be hidden on our property or in his car.

4. The first time he violated one of these conditions he would have to move out of our house for three days. The second violation would result in a week away from our home. The third violation would be a two week suspension. The fourth violation meant that he could no longer live with us at all.

`When Steve saw the consequence of having to move out temporarily, he asked, "But where would I go?" I said, "I don't know. That would be up to you to figure out." He said, "But I could die out there." I answered, "I know. I've considered that possibility. If that happens, I will have to live with it. But this indicates how sure I am that I will not live with a drug addiction being actively practiced in my home, even as sick as you are."

I felt liberated from the Velcro, unhealthy bonds that had tied Steven and me together in a crazy dance ever since his father died. I felt heartbroken, but free. Steven signed the contract.

For a few weeks things went smoothly. Then a day came when he missed a meeting when he was well enough to go. I said that he would have to move out from Friday morning to Sunday evening. Again, he was angry. I packed his medicine and some salt free food in an ice chest and helped him load the chest into his car. I found out later that he spent the weekend at the addict neighbor's house complaining about how awful his mother was. But he stayed clean, and came home Sunday evening rather subdued.

One afternoon a few weeks later, during one of his last hospitalizations to drain fluid collecting around his heart, I was sitting beside his bed, holding his hand, reading a book while I thought he was napping. Without opening his eyes, he began to speak. "Mom, I'm sorry for all the trouble I've caused you. I'm sorry I blamed you and Jim for my problems. I've stopped blaming God for taking my father away from me. The anger is gone. I thought I would just stop using one day and have a normal life. I thought I would marry and have children. I've stopped (using) too late." He went on to describe all the things he loved about his childhood—the vacations we took, the things I let him do, the extended family, cousins he loved, his grandparents." He talked for most of two hours. Somewhere in that outpouring of love he said, "You're the best friend I ever had. The contract I hated has actually helped me stay clean. I know I don't have much longer. I wanted to die with self-respect and the contract is helping me do that. Thank you for doing all you could for me. Thank you for loving me."

The following afternoon as I sat beside him again, I shared with him all of my favorite memories of him…how much I loved being the first one of my family to give birth to a boy, the strength and agility of his little boy body, his daring, his spirit, his loyalty to friends, his kindness to children and animals, his love of his family, his great intelligence and gift of understanding mechanical things, the beauty of the hand-crafted CD holder that was his last gift to me, his belief in my abilities and help with my garden. I told him how proud I was of him for conquering his addiction and how grateful I was that, in these last days, I got to enjoy him as the wonderful, sweet son I had lost fifteen years before, rather than the personality that had been so distorted by drugs.

Mother's Day arrived. He wasn't at all well. His circulation was so poor. His legs were always cold. He was having trouble digesting food. But he wanted to join his grandmother, aunts, uncles and cousins at his cousin's house. When he walked in the door, I could see on everyone's face that they knew this would probably be the last time they saw Steven alive. They gave him a seat in the easy chair, propped up his swollen feet on an ottoman. Although his physical heart was barely functioning, his spiritual heart was wide open to receive all the love they were lavishing on him. Soon, he motioned me that it was time to go.

When we got home, I had to help him up the stairs. He was too short of breath to climb them on his own. While he napped, I arranged to borrow a twin bed to set up downstairs so he would no longer have to climb the stairs. When he saw it, he was so grateful. That night, when

I was ready to go to bed, I hugged him and said, "Good night. I love you!" He asked, "Can I have another hug?" I answered, "You can have as many hugs as you want!"

I asked, "Are you afraid to die?" He answered, "No, I'm not afraid to die. I'm afraid I can't stay clean until I die." Oh, the devilish power of addiction!

We hugged for several more minutes, and finally I said, again, "I love you," and went to bed. I buried my head in my pillow and cried and cried. I didn't think I could bear the pain of losing him.

A few days later, I returned from an errand to find Steven on the kitchen floor, dead. His tired heart had finally stopped. At the last testing, it was three times the size of a normal adult heart and was barely functioning. This physical heart was used up—finished serving this amazing soul… this precious boy and man I'd had the privilege of mothering and through whom I had learned so much.

After calling 911, I sat on the floor with his head in my lap. I said, "You are finally free. The addiction that killed you can no longer touch you. You have finished your time on earth with the self-respect you craved. I bless you as you move on, sweet boy. I will always love you and look forward to seeing you in eternity where there are no tears, no codependency, no addictions, but only pure love." The house felt like it was full of angels, welcoming Steven home.

UPDATE

As time has gone by, my respect and admiration for how Steven lived the last few months of his life have grown. He stopped using speed, cigarettes, marijuana and beer, all at the same time. It's a miracle that, in his weakened state, the detoxing didn't kill him. I knew he'd visited a friend for a few days, but near the end he told me he'd gone there to get through the worst of the hallucinations. At one point, his back was covered with thick, angry looking eruptions as his body fought valiantly to rid itself of all of the accumulated toxins. I am in awe of the courage and fierce determination it took for Steven to kick his addictions…cold turkey. I can barely fathom how consuming and intense his desire to die with self-respect must have been to motivate him through such an incredible feat.

Although the most profound and foundational lessons about recovery from codependency were learned in relationship with Steve, my lessons about recovery are not over. I continue to spot the symptoms in myself in relation to clients, friends and family. When I notice resentment, I must track it to its source and set boundaries. In many other ways, I am learning to make choices that are for my highest good. The process continues of recognizing The Voice and sorting through the messages to allow the ones that serve my good, and change the ones that don't, as I work to heal my own addiction to food.

I, like Steve, hoped that one day the issues with compulsive eating would just disappear and I'd magically regain a healthy weight. This year I faced the reality that it wasn't going to happen without doing the work that Steven did to overcome his addiction. I find that every time I eat when I'm not hungry, every time I eat past fullness, or binge on sweets, it's because I'm using food to escape the insulting, abusive messages from The Voice. Some of the most frequent messages are, "You haven't worked hard enough today. You should have accomplished more. It doesn't matter that you're tired—push through! You're books will never help others. They aren't written well enough. You don't deserve to have your books published. You aren't perfect yet. Try harder! You're all alone in this. It's all up to you. This food will take the tiredness away. Your knee hurts? Well of course it hurts! You're fat!" and on and on it goes.

These messages are so subtle, so insidious, so sneaky. It's hard to tune out the promise of peace calling to me from a chocolate bar with almonds or a big piece of carrot cake and make myself turn up the volume of The Voice so I can clearly hear what is driving me to eat. It's hard to believe that chocolate or carrot cake will not make the shame go away that is the result of The Voice's vicious messages. It's hard to hear and reject accusations that have, perhaps, a smidgen of truth buried in them. It's hard to believe that many of the accusations are out and out lies!

So my journey continues. I'm realizing that while I learned so much about how to have healthier relationships with others, I still have a lot to learn about creating and sustaining a healthy relationship with myself. My conscious self is learning to say in response to The Voice, "Thank you for your good intention, but I've worked enough today. I don't have to try so hard. It's time to rest. I am not alone. The Universe is conspiring for my good! I am living within the circle of ease and grace. I am walking in peace as I'm trusting my path to unfold. Who I am and what I do is enough."

Like Steven, I've found and use a support system that is helping me through this portion of my journey. I have Carrie, a fabulous and empathic life coach. I have Nancy, a gifted and inspiring therapist. I have Melissa, a dear friend who is traveling a similar path. I have my friend Kristi who recently recommended a couple of life-changing books, *The Force of Kindness* by Sharon Salzberg and *Radical Acceptance* by Tara Brach. I have Geneen Roth's book, *Women, Food and God* that helps me identify the road signs for this journey. I have followers who respond to my blog and both share the journey and praise my progress. And I enjoy the friendship of many colleagues in the world of relationship education who are unfailingly supportive.

I also have loved ones who shared my journey for a time and then moved on. They cheer me from the sidelines of heaven. One of them is my beloved son, Steven. It seems fitting to end this chapter with the words I penned to Steven at the beginning of this book:

Dedication
For Steven
You gave me thousands of delightful memories and
taught me more about Codependency and Boundaries
than I thought I needed to know.
I look forward to my next big hug from you!

STIR THE POT: Conquering Codependency and Addiction

I highly recommend you read more about codependency and its role in the unconscious support of destructive behavior. Melody Beattie's book, *Codependent No More*, although written years ago, is still a classic in the field. You may find support at *Codependents Anonymous* meetings, as well. You can look up your local chapter in the phone book or Google the name. Recently, I've been impressed by Dr. Shefali Tsabary's book, *The Conscious Parent: Transforming Ourselves, Empowering Our Children*. She does an outstanding job of helping us as parents identify the dysfunctional motivations that often drive our ineffective parenting methods. She helps parents see themselves and the child from a higher, less ego-centric point of view that allows for more functional parenting. It took me a lifetime to arrive at the parenting place described in her book. James Lehman's program, *The Total Transformation* also offers practical ideas for effective parenting.

If you are struggling with an addiction, there are many free or nearly free self-help groups available. Well known are the Alcoholics Anonymous, Narcotics Anonymous and Over-eaters Anonymous groups. A Christian based version of these recovery principles is called Celebrate Recovery and can be found in many of the larger, local churches. A great book on the topic is *Addiction and Grace: Love and Spirituality in the Healing of Addictions* by Gerald G. May. It's critical that you refuse to believe The Voice when it tells you that you can whip the addiction on your own… that all you need is the right diet, or pill or more will-power. Addictions are incredibly powerful patterns of feelings, thoughts and behaviors that few of us can conquer without on-going support.

SUMMARY OF PUNGENT BOUNDARIES

Most of this book exposes the consequences of codependency in relationship with others. It seems to be ending with the consequences of being codependent with myself—reluctant to face the consequences of my own choices and the challenge of becoming more aware, more conscious, more responsible in ways that support my ultimate wellbeing.

It is my hope that this book has provided understandable explanations and examples of how codependency negatively impacts our relationships with others. Perhaps the surprise ending—the exposure of my own struggles with addiction and irresponsibility—will inspire you to look within for areas where being irresponsible for yourself is hurting you.

I also hope that when you see codependency in your relationships, either with others or within yourself, you will respond with kindness and compassion toward yourself. We are all on a journey of discovery, of growth, of increasing awareness and consciousness. The persons and personal struggles you encounter are there to provoke and support your growth, even though, at the time, the lessons may seem distasteful, or even bitter, like the most pungent brew.

Although the word "pungent" can have a distasteful connotation, I believe it is an apt description of the process of recognizing codependency and setting appropriate boundaries. It's not fun. It's not sweet. I wouldn't wish my lessons on anyone. But the result of adding this brew to my ***Love Potions for Healthy Relationships*** pot has been nothing short of the most amazing healing. I wish for you the same…

Nancy Landrum

YOU ARE INVITED...

Your input is valuable. I'd love it if you'd take the time to post a review of *Pungent Boundaries* on www.Amazon.com or e-mail me personally at Nancy@NancyLandrum.com

Worksheets that are recommended in all the Love Potions volumes are available as a free download at www.NancyLandrum.com They include the Defective Communication Tools Inventory, a comprehensive list of Feeling Words, Planning What to Say, Directions for a Skilled Dialogue and the powerful Problem Solving Worksheet contributed by Mary Ortwein.

*All downloadable documents are copyrighted and may only be duplicated for your personal use.

You may communicate with me via these avenues, or for further relationship insights visit me at:
Blog: www.NancyLandrumblog.com
Website and Monthly Newsletter Sign-up Form: www.nancylandrum.com
Facebook Business Page: NancyLandrumAuthorCoach

If you have a sensitive issue you wish to share with me, a "private message" option is available on all three sites. I am the only one who sees those messages and will personally respond.

I currently provide private coaching as well as occasional relationship workshops for those who are near the Inland Empire in Southern California. I also offer weekend Relationship Intensives for couples who live too far away to attend regular workshops or coaching. Check out current options at www.NancyLandrum.com

When complete, this series of seven small books will give you the primary ingredients to concoct your own *Love Potions for Healthy*

Relationships. If you sign up to receive my newsletter or blogs, you'll be among the first to hear about the publishing of the next *Love Potions* books. As each volume is published, my followers will be given a bargain price for a limited time.

Preview: SUCCESSFUL SOLUTIONS FOR STEPFAMILIES

"Ladies and Gentlemen, we are gathered here together
To join this man and this woman in holy matrimony..."
Opening words to Jim and Nancy Landrum's wedding ceremony.

Most, if not all, marriages begin with blissful confidence surrounded by a soft cloud of romantic love and sexual energy. Ours was no different. We were euphoric. We didn't have a clue that a few short years later the paragraph below would describe our relationship.

> Divorce! The word shattered the space and hung in the air between us like a red fog. Even after all the conflict we'd experienced, we were both stunned to silence by the introduction of that possibility. How could our relationship have come to this? Why wasn't it enough to love each other? We'd always heard that love and commitment were all it took to have a great marriage. We *did* love each other. We were *very* committed to each other and to our marriage. What was wrong? We'd both been through so much and were so happy to find each other. We were in our forties. Adults. Why couldn't we resolve the conflicts that were eating away at our love and commitment like a deadly cancer?

The words above form the opening paragraph of ***How to Stay Married & Love It! Solving the Puzzle of a SoulMate Marriage***, a book my late husband Jim and I wrote. In it we describe our journey of finding the communication and conflict management skills that resurrected the love we'd nearly lost. Those same skills are also applied to a variety of relationship examples in the *Love Potions for Healthy Relationships* series.

Jim and I adopted more rational beliefs about relationships as described in *Season the Pot*. We learned and practiced the speaking and listening skills shared in *Communication Elixirs*. We gained mastery over our destructive emotions in order to maintain respect for each other 24/7 using the strategies outlined in *Savory Safeguards*. And we equalized the sharing of responsibilities taught in *Pungent Boundaries.* All of these skills were *essential* to stop the fighting… halt the downward spiral…but they weren't enough to help us resolve the main conflict. We didn't know it at the time, but we also desperately needed to understand the fundamental differences in dynamics between first families and stepfamilies in order to find a workable solution to our issue.

OUR STEPFAMILY STORY

After only four and one half years, my first marriage ended abruptly when I was only twenty-three years old with the unexpected death of my husband. I had a two boys, Steven who was two years old, and Peter who was eight months old. I was a single mom for thirteen years.

A mutual friend introduced me to Jim, a widower whose wife died after a protracted illness. He had three children: Teri who had married Greg a few months before I met Jim; Karen, a seventeen-year-old senior in high school; and Jimmy, his eight year old son.

We began dating casually and became good friends, gradually falling in love. Our many friends and family members celebrated our wedding with us in the Spring of 1981. We had each survived the loss of a spouse, were responsible, caring persons, and were sure that we were due for some better times. We had no doubt that we were meant to be together. After celebrating our wedding vows, we blissfully left for a two-week honeymoon.

Before we married we agreed to continue single-parenting our teens. We figured that they were at the worst possible age to accept a new parental figure…a choice that has been validated by stepfamily research. But we both wanted Jim's young son, Jimmy, to have the benefit of two parents. The day we returned from our honeymoon, the conflict began. We had very different styles of parenting, and our ideas about what Jimmy needed were miles apart.

Years later we heard that this is an issue that is common for many step-couples. Our hurtful communication methods exacerbated the conflict as we each grew more entrenched in our respective positions. The areas of safety between us began shrinking as the area of conflict expanded. We began to lose hope. Each of us secretly feared our marriage had been a terrible mistake.

In spite of our disenchantment, we didn't want to give up. Jim and I began an intense search for help. It slowly came in small pieces…a suggestion here, a concept there…until we found a lay coach who taught us the rudiments of the communication guidelines outlined in the first **How to…** book and refined in **Communication Elixirs** and **Savory Safeguards**. As mentioned before, those skills stopped the crazy fights, and enabled us to manage our anger more respectfully, but didn't resolve our issue. Our coach finally made a suggestion that was shocking to us, and painful to implement, but turned out to be a successful solution.

REAL SOLUTIONS FROM REAL STEPFAMILIES

In addition to some illustrations from my own stepfamily, in this volume you will meet several step-couples, and a few of their children, hear their struggles, and learn from their successful solutions.

Gavin and Pamela: I met Gavin and Pamela at a program preview where I was given 15 minutes to "plug" my *Mastering the Mysteries of Stepfamilies* class. I identified them as a step-couple as they avidly listened to my spiel. When the meeting was dismissed, they practically jumped over chairs to get to me. With tears running down their cheeks, they shared their desperation. As I'd shared about Jim's and my issue about parenting at the preview, they thought, "Finally someone knows what we're going through. Maybe she can help us."

A few days later I met with them in private. Two hours later they left with a practical solution that immediately moved them from desperate to hopeful. When the class began a few weeks later, they diligently listened, were open to new concepts, and faithfully practiced new skills. Last year I had the privilege of conducting their vow-renewal ceremony for their seventh anniversary. They shared that now they know they will be able to keep their commitment to each other until death parts them. And, they are thoroughly enjoying each other and their respective children.

For Father's Day last year, Gavin received a letter from his early-twenties step-son thanking him for the work he saw Gavin do to learn how to love Pamela better, and for the changes he made in order to preserve their floundering stepfamily. After being abandoned by his birth father *and* his first step-father, for the first time in this boy's life, he was seeing a healthy, loving marriage relationship.

Amanda: The daughter of Pamela (above) poignantly shares what it has been like for her to be a child with a birth-father, (who had been physically abusive to Pamela and gave up his parental rights to avoid paying child support) and the first stepfather who mostly ignored her while drinking in the garage. When her mother married Gavin, the hope of a loving family soon disintegrated into fighting between all of the members. As a thirteen year old, she poignantly asked, "What is my name?" expressing the confusion of having three fathers, three last names. Amanda and other children in stepfamilies will share their touching perspectives of what stepfamily life is like from the children's point of view.

Skip and Wendy: Skip and Wendy were each previously divorced. They had seven half-grown children between them. They fell in love and set the date for their wedding. They attended a marriage prep class designed specifically for potential stepfamilies. They were determined that this marriage would last, so in addition to the stepfamily class, they saw a therapist that helped them understand their personality and gender differences. Somewhere in that preparation, they realized they were not ready to join households successfully. There were too many potential conflicts for which they were unprepared. They postponed the wedding for a year…a year they both agree was one of the hardest they'd ever experienced. They not only had significant differences in parenting, but also some major financial issues to work out.

Today they are not only a shining example of successful stepfamily solutions, but generously share their experience by teaching a nationally known program in their local church. *Designing Dynamic Stepfamilies* is a video based program by Gordon and Carrie Taylor. (www.designingdynamicstepfamilies.com) Hundreds of couples have benefitted from Kip and Wendy's willingness to share the lessons they learned.

Charles and Susan: Susan was so discouraged by the lack of resources and support for second or subsequent marriages, that she heads up a business that acts as a clearing house for appropriate information and services. Shortly after marrying, Susan and her husband Charles discovered that his family was noticeably cool toward her and her two boys. The attitude demonstrated was that Susan's children were not their *real* grandchildren. What they encountered is another frequent stepfamily issue—the lack of acceptance of the "new" family. In addition, Charles and Susan had conflicting ideas about how much support to give their respective children as they prepared for college expenses.

Ken and Irma: When Ken and Irma married, they vowed that they would never, under any circumstances, put themselves or their children through the pain of another divorce. Yet a few years later they were maintaining their commitment to not divorce, but living separately under the same roof. Participants in the classes and couples' retreats that they now teach laugh when Ken and Irma describe how even the refrigerator was divided in half with black electricians' tape! This inspiring couple eventually learned some simple communication and conflict management skills that transformed their relationship. Ken and Irma attended my *Mastering the Mysteries of Stepfamilies* course as participants and then co-taught that curriculum with me. They, and the refrigerator, are no longer divided. In fact they help lead a non-profit support group for couples in distress (*The Third Option*, a national program) and teach marriage retreats for couples who want more from their marriage.

Nathan: Nathan came to one of my classes because he was reared in a stepfamily and wanted to better understand the relentless conflict he experienced. He left with much more compassion for his mom and step-dad, as well as great relief that he could release much of the anger and guilt he felt, believing he might have been at fault.

Don and Kim: Don and Kim attended my *Mastering the Mysteries of Stepfamilies* class when they were just beginning the journey of combining their families. They diligently learned and practiced the communication and conflict management skills they learned there. Maintaining respectful communication with Don's Ex, has been especially challenging, but a goal that he works hard to maintain as they negotiate custody and visitation issues. Kim felt drawn to her young step-daughter Deanna and invested a lot of time and energy into building a good relationship with her. When, as a result of the birth mother's jealousy, Deanna chose to end the close relationship with her step-mother, Kim was crushed. Because Kim was so much more emotionally stable than the birth mother, Kim made a typical stepfamily assumption that she, with caring and compassion, would command the loyalty due a *real* mother from Deanna.

This volume of the ***Love Potions for Healthy Relationship*** series uses real stories from these and other step-couples' experiences to demonstrate the practicality and power of ***Successful Stepfamily Solutions***.

SUCCESSFUL STEPFAMILY EXPECTATIONS

From the beginning of time, the general belief has been that a stepfamily could (and should) function the same as a first family. Thankfully, some courageous researchers took on that assumption, and, after extensively interviewing thousands of step-couples, discovered that stepfamilies who were optimally successful employed out-of-the-box solutions that wouldn't be characteristic of a first family. On the other hand, step-couples whose marriages did not survive the stress of "blending," were often attempting to fit the square peg of a stepfamily into the round hole of a first family model.

My definition of a successful stepfamily is one in which the husband and wife are committed to learning and using respectful communication skills with each other, their children, and stepchildren. Their expectations are realistic. Solutions to issues accommodate the stepfamily dynamic. The marriage is strong and loving. Honor is given to the other living or deceased biological parents and extended family. The children feel safe, cared for, and respected by the adults in their lives and their stepsiblings.

Comprehensive lists of *Building Blocks* and *Stumbling Blocks* to success will be shared in the following chapters. These lists are gleaned directly from research that identified solutions to common stepfamily issues that work for the most successful stepfamilies.

A LOVE POTION FOR STEPFAMILIES

In keeping with my theme of a **Love Potion**, a "solution" is a mixture of two or more chemicals which remain distinctly separate, even when mixed together. They do not interact with each other to form a new chemical. They remain separate, even when sharing the same container.

A stepfamily is like a chemical solution, in that three or more persons are mixed together but each remains a separate identity. There is no magic appliance that automatically "blends" a new family that is loving and happy. We are not milkshakes. That is why, although the term is not ideal, I continue to use the name "stepfamily" to designate any family in which one or both partners have a child from a previous relationship.

Another meaning of "solution" is a proposed action that *may* meet a need or resolve a problem. A stepfamily solution may be proposed to resolve a conflict, but some solutions, often ones based on the model of a first family, fail the parent, the marriage or the children. A *Successful Stepfamily Solution* is a way of resolving an issue or conflict that, over time, proves itself to work for all persons involved.

SUMMARY

Today's couples expect a much higher degree of satisfaction with their relationship than couples in previous centuries. Today, persons "couple" based on the magic of falling in love, believing that their love alone will enable them to resolve all issues that may arise. In addition to new love, step-couples bring wounds from past losses and fierce determination to make this new relationship succeed. Most couples, step- or not, haven't had the opportunity to learn the powerful skills that would help them build a long-lasting, satisfying partnership. Even less well known is that a stepfamily works differently than a first family and requires different solutions in order to be successful over time for both the adults and the children. This book provides insight about what works and what doesn't based on known research outcomes and the real-world experiences of several couples.

STIR THE POT: Examine Expectations
What circumstances led to your participation in a stepfamily? What were your expectations about how your stepfamily would function? What benefits did you expect to receive from a new partner? How did you think your relationship with a step-child would be like? What did you expect from your new spouse in regard to your child/ren? What has surprised you? Were the child/ren's attitudes different before the marriage took place? How have they changed? What issues are you experiencing that you hope to get new insight about from this book?

ABOUT NANCY'S WORK...

Nancy, with her late husband Jim, taught their marriage skills workshops to hundreds of couples in locations throughout California. Since his passing, Nancy has continued to teach the skills that gave Nancy and Jim the marriage of their dreams.

Nancy has presented several workshops, particularly about step-family strategies, at the national *Smart Marriages Conference* and *National Association of Relationship and Marriage Education.* (NARME) Two couples' stories of being coached back from the brink of divorce have been featured in the national magazine, *FIRST for Women.*

In 2010, Nancy was invited by Mary Ortwein, the author of *Mastering the Mysteries of Love*, to adapt that relationship skills program for use with stepfamilies. *Mastering the Mysteries of Stepfamilies* has been successful in helping many stepfamily couples adapt relationship strategies to their unique needs.

In 2011, Nancy republished the stepfamilies strategies portion into a program called *Stepping TwoGether: Building a Strong Stepfamily.* This curriculum is designed to be used as an add-on program to any good communication skills program.

In addition to the seven volumes in the ***Love Potions for Healthy Relationships*** series, she intends to write a book specifically in support of parents of drug addicted children.

Her monthly newsletter and weekly blogs give insight and support to those who seek information leading to healthier relationships with others, as well as better self-care. (See You Are Invited...) She enjoys coaching private clients in the studio behind her home in Murrieta, CA or via phone or Skype.

Books by Nancy Landrum
Written with her late SoulMate, Jim Landrum:
How to Stay Married & Love It! Solving the Puzzle of a SoulMate Marriage,
River Publishing, 2002, 2012
How to Stay Married & Love It EVEN MORE! Completing the Puzzle of a SoulMate Marriage,
River Publishing, 2012
Both "How to…" books are available on Amazon.com

TESTIMONIALS from the "How to…" books:
"This book changed my life…it is about marriage but in essence it's about YOU and how your attitude impacts the relationship. When you change you will see the changes around you. Nancy and Jim Landrum did a fabulous job in writing this book. I highly recommend it even if you are not having difficulty in your marriage." Susan Kay Johnson's review on Amazon.com

"I gave my copy of your book to one of my good friends who was about as close to divorce as you can get without actually filing for one. I was telling her about the book and she said she didn't think anything would help at this point and guess what? I saw them at a party last weekend and they were talking, hugging and kissing…she loves, loves, loves the book and was so thankful that I 'made' her read it. I also had a student writing an essay about marriage. I lent him (your) book. He said there were so many quotes he was having a hard time choosing which ones to use!" Susan Johnson-Royce, Therapist, Minnesota

"The chapter on listening is the most powerful chapter I've ever read in any book." Felicia Mannion, Murrieta, CA

TESTIMONIALS AND REVIEWS:
Season the Pot teaches how unconscious beliefs may determine the poor quality of relationships we experience. Steps for successfully changing old beliefs into beliefs that serve healthier relationship goals are included. One reviewer said, "As a seasoned clinical therapist in the mental health field, I have read many relationship books. What I appreciate about Nancy's perspective is that she is writing to the

ordinary person struggling with a relationship and not to other mental health professionals. Her belief in the power of positive relationships is contagious and her ability to present her ideas in a simple to follow 'recipe' makes it easy to dive in."

Melissa Marrs, LCSW Copyright 2013

"Keep writing! Your words are like something sweet on warm bread. They are so gentle and yet real; they just soak in, almost undetectably. Thank you!" Traci Carman

"Nancy Landrum has taken those things in life that tend to trip us up in our marriage relationship and unpacked them in a way that will help couples move forward in their relationship. *Season the Pot* is an easy read filled with one golden nugget after the other. Found myself relating to many of the personal stories in the book and LOVED the way she incorporated the tools all of us need and can learn to make our marriages thrive."

Julie M Baumgardner, President and CEO of First Things First

Communication Elixirs:
(This book) clearly guides you through the simple steps of replacing communication methods that separate, with communication methods that connect. "What a gem! Through my work I have read tons of books on Communications and Relationships, so I can say with confidence that Nancy Landrum has done a masterful job of presenting the best research-based communication practices in a way that anyone can understand and implement in their most important relationships."
Dennis Stoica, founder of Healthy Relationships California.

"Every relationship struggles now and then when it comes to communication. Nancy Landrum has done a masterful job with ***Communication Elixirs*** providing a whole host of helpful tools to help couples enhance their communication and take their relationship to the next level. It's a quick read and worth every minute."

Julie M. Baumgardner, President and CEO of First Things First and Board Chair, National Association for Relationship and Marriage Education.

Savory Safeguards, available May, 2014:
"Overpowering emotions? Recurrent problems? Nancy Landrum, M.A., reveals how to break the painful cycle of hurt in this 3rd volume of her ***Love Potions for Healthy Relationship*** series, ***Savory Safeguards.*** By following the simple steps outlined in this book, one has the keys to rebuilding themselves and their relationships with lasting change. Landrum has brilliantly helped transform the lives of so many people.... this book will no doubt change the lives of many more!"

-Sylvia Palda, M.S., M.A., LMFT. Founder of Aspire Psychotherapy & Counseling, www.aspirefamilytherapy.com. Clinical Outreach Specialist for Healthy Relationships California, a non-profit committed to educating the world with healthy relationships skills.

"We love this book! As you read ***Savory Safeguards***, you'll become enchanted by Nancy's ability to teach a relationship concept clearly and concisely, and then tell a story which not only grabs you, but also illustrates the concept perfectly! There is so much here to help protect and grow a healthy relationship, from research-based strategies for managing strong emotions, to practical steps for finding solutions that work, to inspiration and encouragement for those who feel like they're the only ones working at the relationship. We heartily recommend reading - and *savoring* - this book!"

Don & Alex Flecky, co-authors of *CoupleTalk*, www.coupletalk.com

"I often hear couples say, 'We just don't know how to communicate.' I beg to differ. I think couples are definitely communicating, but *how* they are communicating is impacting their relationship in profound ways. Nancy Landrum has done a fabulous job of breaking down how couples can communicate in a way that builds up their relationship instead of tearing it down. LOVED the way she incorporated the tools all of us need to help marriages thrive!"

Julie M Baumgardner, President and CEO of First Things First Board Chair, National Association for Relationship and Marriage Education

Pungent Boundaries available Fall, 2014

"Nancy Landrum's *Pungent Boundaries* is an informative and helpful short manual to enable the reader to explore co-dependency and steps in the path of setting boundaries within such relationships. It is filled with many helpful vignettes along with exceptional transparency on the part of the author in relating her own life and journey. I found the metaphor used in Chapter 4 to be especially insightful in understanding co-dependency. The focus of this guide in on what the reader can do and not on the partner in the relationship."

Arthur L Prescott, PhD (Retired), School Psychologist
Adjunct Professor in graduate clinical and counseling programs, Rosemead School of Psychology & Point Loma Nazarene University

"Humorous with illustrations right out of our everyday lives, Nancy illustrates the tension between codependency and caring. Easy to read, but not always easy to practice, Nancy will walk you through the construction of your own healthy personal boundaries. The Stir the Pot section after each chapter will keep you honest and happy that you took the time to read this little book!"

Dave Carder
Author of *Torn Asunder: Recovering from an Extramarital Affair*
Pastor, Counseling Ministries, Evangelical Free Church, Fullerton, CA

"Insightful, informative and written with subject matter knowledge, as well as relevant personal information. A good read!"

Dr. Robert Morwood, Professor Emeritus, Point Loma Nazarene University,
Licensed Marriage, Family Therapist

The balance of the ***Love Potions*** series is expected to be complete by the end of 2014.

FEEDBACK FROM COACHING CLIENTS

"I feel such a sense of relief to finally be at a turning point and am ready for the work ahead. I am very grateful for all the gentle guidance you've given us." Barb Sisson, Aurora, CA

"Me and my wife, Alicia, took one of your classes during a very rocky period in our marriage. Our marriage (now) is stronger than ever. You were so generous with your time and expertise, and patient with us as we crawled through the valley. Keep up the very important work." Chris Cole, Brea, CA

"Nancy Landrum helped our marriage when we were in the midst of despair. She shared guidelines for step-families that became our life preservers. Almost immediately our storms began to calm. Nancy coached us on many occasions and was there when we made amazing discoveries about ourselves and one another. Each coaching session felt safe and relaxing even if the topics were difficult. Nancy was able to see how much we loved each other at a time when we were so deep in our troubles we couldn't see. In July, 2012, Nancy performed our vow renewal and because of her, our vows meant more this time than they did the first time." Pamela and Gavin Fenske, Fullerton, CA

A BLOG READER'S POST

"Do you need change? Do you need a place to go to read encouraging words? If so please 'like' my dear sweet friend Nancy Landrum Author Coach Facebook page and subscribe to her blog. I don't know how she does it but each time I read her blog it seems to apply directly to me ...selfishly, I just tell myself she is just writing to ME ME ME. Here is today's blog...enjoy!" Kathy T.

MORE ABOUT THE AUTHOR

At a very young age, Nancy decided she would write books to help others have happy, loving relationships. She had no idea where that journey would take her or how strenuous the lessons would be. The road eventually led to a Masters Degree in Psychology. Her life-long hunger continues as she learns more about the ingredients of healthy relationships. She enjoys sharing the powerful results of her search through writing, speaking, teaching and private coaching in her backyard Studio.

Currently, two pups named Max and Toby welcome her as their caretakers in a home on a semi-desert half-acre in Southern California. Nancy, Max and Toby are frequently entertained by the quirky behavior of six hens, known as "the girls." Lessons from all the critters and her gardening are occasionally featured in a blog. She optimistically hopes she can tame the dirt and weeds into a refuge of beauty and peace without raising her water bill through the roof. (She's given up taming Max, Toby or "the girls"!) Temperatures range from 10° F to 110° F, so finding plants that survive both extremes is proving difficult!

Nancy does her best to bring balance to her life with family, friends, fiercely competitive table games, exercise, visits to the farmers market for organic produce, gardening, drawing book illustrations, an occasional sewing project, and painting anything from a piece of furniture to her wide, white front porch. She recently bought a miter saw in order to build some things she's envisioned for her garden.